# The
# Canadian Forces Aptitude Test
### (CFAT) Study Guide

Complete Review & Test Prep With 180+
Official Style Practice Questions & Answers

*Written by Fred Winstone*

# Disclaimer & Copyright:

## © COPYRIGHT 2023 Fred Winstone – All Rights Reserved

The content contained within this book may not be reproduced, duplicated or transmitted without direct written permission from the author or the publisher. Under no circumstances will any blame or legal responsibility be held against the publisher, or author, for any damages, reparation, or monetary loss due to the information contained within this book. Either directly or indirectly. You are responsible for your own choices, actions, and results.

**This book is in the process of attaining copyright certification from the US Copyright Office, at the Library of Congress. For information on the registration number, contact the publisher.**

*Cover Image Licensed by Freepik.com: Account # 56ebd41d-19d4-444c-a966-d86168186415*

### Legal Notice:

This book is copyright protected. This book is only for personal use. You cannot amend, distribute, sell, use, quote or paraphrase any part, or the content within this book, without the consent of the author or publisher.

### Disclaimer Notice:

Please note the information contained within this document is for educational and entertainment purposes only. All effort has been executed to present accurate, up to date, and reliable, complete information. No warranties of any kind are declared or implied. Readers acknowledge that the author is not engaging in the rendering of legal, financial, medical or professional advice. The content within this book has been derived from various sources, as well as the author's personal experience. Please consult a licensed professional before attempting any techniques outlined in this book.

By reading this document, the reader agrees that under no circumstances is the author or publisher responsible for any losses, direct or indirect, which are incurred as a result of the use of the information contained within this document, including, but not limited to, — errors, omissions, or inaccuracies.

# Table of Contents

Disclaimer & Copyright: ............................................................. 3

Introduction ................................................................................ 5

Chapter 1: Why Take the CFAT? ............................................. 8

Chapter 2: Exam Information ................................................ 10

Chapter 3: Verbal Skills ........................................................... 15

Chapter 4: Spatial Ability ........................................................ 23

Chapter 5: Problem Solving ................................................... 27

Chapter 6: Personality Inventory ......................................... 53

Chapter 7: Practice Test 1 ....................................................... 55

Chapter 8: Practice Test 2 ....................................................... 75

Chapter 9: Practice Test 3 ...................................................... 94

Chapter 10: Practice Test 1 Answers with Explanations ............................................................................ 113

Chapter 11: Practice Test 2 Answers With Explanations ............................................................................ 146

Chapter 12: Practice Test 3 Answers With Explanations ............................................................................ 177

Conclusion ................................................................................ 208

# Introduction

The Canadian Armed Forces provides a broad range of career opportunities. Whether you are interested in the Army, Navy, or Air Force, there are many ways to be involved in serving your country through defensive and humanitarian efforts. Before you can become a part of this long tradition of national service, however, you must pass the CFAT.

The Canadian Forces Aptitude Test (CFAT) is an entrance exam required of all applicants to the Canadian Armed Forces. The CFAT tests your aptitude in verbal skills, spatial ability, and problem-solving. This exam is one way that the Armed Forces screens its applicants to ensure that recruits are competent and capable, ready to serve in the critical and challenging roles the military has available.

Preparing for the CFAT can seem like a daunting task. The test is complex, and the study resources available are sparse. Students often aren't sure how to study, and many of the limited resources online just recycle the same questions, so there aren't many unique questions to practice.

We're here to help. This book will equip you with everything you need to be successful on the CFAT. With thorough content review, proven test-taking strategies, and plenty of original practice questions, this book will guide you as you prepare for your testing day.

First, this book will give you an overview of the CFAT. Chapters 1 and 2 will provide information about the test's content, format, eligibility requirements, scoring, and more. We want you to have all the information you read at your fingertips, so you don't have to search all over the internet to find out what you need. With this guide, you'll know what to expect on testing day.

Next, Chapters 3-5 will outline what you will encounter on each of the three CFAT subtests. We'll cover content and strategies for Verbal Skills, Spatial Ability, and Problem Solving. Chapter 6 will walk you through what to expect from the Personality Inventory accompanying the CFAT.

Finally, you will find three full-length practice tests in Chapter 7 to help you feel fully prepared for the real thing. Chapter 8 contains the answers to these practice tests with complete explanations, so you can learn from what you got right and wrong to improve your future performance.

If you are ready to put in the time and effort to study, this book will give you all the tools and practice you need to succeed. Make good use of these resources—study each chapter thoroughly, take all three practice tests, and read the explanations for every question—and you will be well-prepared for the CFAT. We are eager to help you get ready for the exam that will help launch your military career. Let's go to the first chapter and begin!

# Chapter 1:
# Why Take the CFAT?

The Canadian Forces Aptitude Test (CFAT) is an exam the Canadian Armed Forces uses to screen candidates for enlistment and job placement. It assesses a range of skills, including vocabulary, logic, spatial reasoning, mathematical knowledge, and problem-solving. The CFAT is an essential early step toward a military career.

A career in the Canadian Armed Forces has many benefits. In addition to the honour of serving your country, a military career can offer unique experiences and learning opportunities. The CAF offers paid education programs, competitive salaries and benefits, and even has dedicated programs for Indigenous Peoples. Military service can also develop discipline, physical fitness, technical skills, and leadership abilities to improve your future in and out of the military. Opportunities for travel, camaraderie, and meaningful work are among the many reasons people join the armed forces.

Joining the Armed Forces might be the **world's greatest adventure**, and one that I revere to this day. You'll get the chance to make a solid group of friends, some of who you'll surely know for the rest of your life. It's not the easiest job in the world, but nothing worth having comes easy. To serve Canada is an honor and a privilege.

Anyone interested in joining the armed forces–Regular or Reserve Force– must take and pass the CFAT, but the exam does more than just determine who is eligible to join. It is also part of the process used to determine which candidates will be best suited for which positions within the military.

The enlistment process is very competitive, so doing your best on the CFAT will increase your chances of acceptance into your chosen branch and career path. We're here to help you with that process. Turn to Chapter 2, and let's learn more about the specifics of the CFAT.

# Chapter 2: Exam Information

Now, we'll look at the specifics of the CFAT. In this chapter, we'll cover how to take the test, its format, and its scoring.

## How to Take the CFAT

Before you take the CFAT, you should be aware of the other eligibility requirements for enlistment in the armed forces. To join the CAF, you must:
- be between the ages of 16 and 57 years old (applicants under 18 must have parental consent)
- be a Canadian citizen or permanent resident
- have completed grade 10 (or attained 24 credits of Secondary IV in Quebec); to enter as an officer, you must have completed grade 12 (Secondary V in Quebec) and have or be working towards a Bachelor's degree
- pass a medical screening, which includes a physical exam and a medical history file review

Additionally, as part of the enlistment process, you will be asked to complete an application, reliability screening, and interview.

Your application process starts with an online application and screening (https://forces.ca/en/apply-now).
Once you have completed this step and submitted all required documentation, a CAF recruiter will contact you to schedule an appointment to take the CFAT at one of the Canadian Forces Recruiting Centres (CFRC). The CFAT is available in English and French, so be sure to tell your recruiter which language you prefer to test in when you make your appointment.

When you go to your testing appointment, you must bring the following:
- Canadian government-issued photo identification, such as a driver's license or passport
- Proof of Canadian citizenship or permanent residency (PR) status, such as a birth certificate, citizenship certificate, or permanent resident card
- Official academic transcripts from your high school and college (if applicable)

If you do not bring these documents with you, you may not be permitted to take the test that day, delaying your application process.

## Test Format

The CFAT consists entirely of multiple-choice questions with four possible answer choices and only one correct answer. The CFAT includes three subtests:
- **Verbal Skills** assesses your vocabulary.

- **Spatial Ability** is an image-based test that evaluates your spatial reasoning skills.
- **Problem Solving** is a test of basic mathematics and logical reasoning.

The following chart shows the length and number of questions on each subtest.

| Subtest | # of Questions | Time Limit |
| --- | --- | --- |
| Verbal Skills | 15 | 5 minutes |
| Spatial Ability | 15 | 10 minutes |
| Problem Solving | 30 | 45 minutes |
| **TOTAL** | **60 questions** | **60 minutes** |

Calculators or other devices are not permitted on any part of the exam. You will be given blank paper and a pencil for calculations or other notes.

After the main CFAT, you will also be given a personality inventory assessment. This is used to determine whether your personality is likely to be a good fit for the position(s) you are applying for. We'll discuss this assessment in more detail in Chapter 6.

# CFAT Scoring and Results

Your CFAT scores will compare your results to those of other applicants. There are minimum score requirements for acceptance into each CAF branch and for qualifying for specific military occupations. The

CAF has made very little information about the CFAT scoring process public, including the minimum cutoff scores for acceptance. Recruiters are not even required to tell you the exact score you received after you've taken the test.

What they will do, however, is go over the implications of your test results with you. Once your test is scored, a recruiter will discuss with you your career options based on both your test results and your educational background. Then, you will select up to three occupations you are interested in applying for. If selected for enlistment, the CAF will process you for one of these three occupations based on both the current needs of the CAF and your qualification relative to other applicants.

If your CFAT scores do not qualify you for enlistment, or if they are not high enough to qualify you for a specific occupation you are interested in, you may retake the test after a waiting period of one month. You can request a retest from the recruiting centre where you applied. After taking the test a second time, if your score is still insufficient, you may take the test a third and final time. Before taking the third attempt, however, you must submit proof that you have completed an academic course related to the skills tested on the CFAT in the period since you previously took the exam. CFAT scores do not expire, so there is no maximum time limit on when you can rewrite the exam. Ensure you are well-prepared before making another testing appointment since your third try is your last chance.

Now that you're acquainted with the logistics of the CFAT, let's dive into its content. In the next three chapters, we'll look at what is covered on each of the CFAT subtests and how you can achieve your best score.

# Chapter 3: Verbal Skills

The first section of the CFAT is Verbal Skills. You will have 5 minutes to answer 15 questions. It is a fast-paced assessment of your grasp of vocabulary.

## Verbal Skills Question Types

There are three main question types on the Verbal Skills subtest: synonyms, antonyms, and word analogies.

### Synonym Questions

Definition questions are the most common type. In these questions, you will be given a word and asked to select the word from among the four answer choices that is most similar in meaning. Most of these questions will follow the format of this example:

1. INCONSEQUENTIAL means the same as
    A. effective
    B. disorganized
    C. advantageous
    D. unimportant

The correct answer here is (D), since both *inconsequential* and *unimportant* refer to something insignificant.

A few synonym questions may ask you to complete a sentence that gives a little more context to the word, but you still solve them the same way—by finding the word that most closely matches the meaning of the uppercase word. Here's an example:

2. An ALTRUISTIC person is
   A. generous
   B. selfish
   C. intelligent
   D. cunning

Here, you are looking for another way to describe an *altruistic* person by finding a synonym for that word. Choice (A), *generous*, is the best match.

## Antonym Questions

You may come across an occasional antonym question. These look very similar to synonym questions, except they ask you for a word that means the opposite of the given word. Here's an example:

3. MUNDANE is the opposite of
   A. studious
   B. exciting
   C. angry
   D. boring

*Mundane* means dull or uninteresting, so the opposite of that would be *exciting*, choice (B). Be sure to read questions carefully so that you know whether to look for a synonym or an antonym. One of the wrong answer choices in an antonym question will often be a synonym for the given word. In the example above, notice that choice (D), *boring*, is a synonym for *mundane*. Be careful not to select a synonym when the question asks for the opposite or vice versa.

## Word Analogies

The final type of question on the Verbal Skills subtest is word analogies. These are often the most difficult for many people to master, but by looking at their most common variations and getting in lots of practice, you can get used to these and answer them more confidently.

Word analogy questions present you with three words. The first two words are in relationship to each other. You need to discern what that relationship is, then select the word from among the answer choices that has that same relationship to the third word given. They will follow the format:
"WORD 1 is to WORD 2 as WORD 3 is to" and your job is to select the best "WORD 4" from among the answer choices to complete the analogy. Let's start with a simple example.

4. HOT is to COLD as LIGHT is to
   A. warm
   B. dark
   C. bright
   D. empty

Look at the first two words—*hot* and *cold*. What is the relationship between them? They are opposites. The third word given is *light*, so what you must now look for in the answer choices is the opposite of *light*. The best match is choice (B), *dark*.

You will come across five common word relationships in most analogy questions. If you learn to look out for these relationships, you'll find greater success with these questions. The five most common word relationships are:
1. Opposites
2. Synonyms
3. Description
4. Part-to-Whole
5. Degree of Intensity

We already saw an example of an opposites question. Let's take a look at a synonym analogy.

   5. INTELLIGENT is to SMART as AMIABLE is to
      A. ignorant
      B. assertive
      C. reserved
      D. Friendly

*Intelligent* and *smart* are synonyms, so you need to find a synonym for *amiable* among the answer choices. The best match is choice (D), *friendly*.

Descriptions are another type of word relationship. In these questions, one word in the pair is a noun, and the other is either an adjective describing what the noun is like or a verb describing what the noun does. Take a look at this example.

6. PHILANTHROPIST is to GENEROUS as ARITST is to
    A. stingy
    B. ordinary
    C. creative
    D. painting

A *philanthropist* is someone who is, by definition, *generous* in their support of the welfare of others. Likewise, an *artist* is a person who is *creative*, choice (C). Notice that choice (D), *painting*, can also be related to an artist, but it is not an adjective to describe the artist, like generous is an adjective to describe the philanthropist.

The next type of word relationship is part-to-whole. In these questions, one word in the pair will constitute a part of a larger group, object, or system. Here's an example.

7. PHOTOGRAPH is to ALBUM as BOOK is to
    A. page
    B. library
    C. author
    D. manuscript

A *photograph* is part of a larger collection contained within an *album*. Likewise, a *book* is part of a larger collection of books contained within a *library*, choice (B). This question is a great example of why you need to read carefully and that the order of the words in an analogy pair matters. *Book* and *page*, choice (A), also have a part-whole relationship, but the order is reversed. In the photograph-album relationship, the first word (*photograph*) is the part contained within the whole (*album*), so in the second pair, *book* must represent the part and the correct answer, *library*, must be the whole. On the contrary, *book* is the whole within which the part (*page*) is contained; since this is the reverse order of the first pair, it cannot be correct. (Note: The part is not always listed first; in some questions, the whole may come first in the pair.)

The final type of common analogy is the degree of intensity. In these pairs, one word will have a similar meaning to the other but will be more extreme. For example, *hilarious* is a more extreme version of *amusing*–both mean funny, but hilarious much more so. Let's try an example.

8. LARGE is to GIGANTIC as HUNGRY is to
    A. ravenous
    B. satisfied
    C. enormous
    D. thirsty

The correct answer here is choice (A). *Gigantic* is very *large*; likewise, *ravenous* is very *hungry*.

# Verbal Skills Strategies

Here are some general tips to help you succeed on the Verbal Skills subtest.

1. Practice, practice, practice! The more questions you try ahead of time, the more comfortable you will be with answering them. This is especially true for word analogies questions. Getting used to identifying the relationships between words is key. Three full-length tests in Chapter 7 will give you many opportunities to practice.

2. Read the question stem carefully to ensure you are looking for the right thing. If the question asks for an opposite, be careful not to choose a synonym.

3. In word analogies, pay close attention to the part of speech (whether a word is a noun, verb, adjective, etc.). Corresponding words in the analogy pairs will always have the same part of speech. If WORD 1 is to WORD 2 as WORD 3 is to [WORD 4], Words 1 and 3 will always be the same part of speech, and words 2 and 4 will be the same part of speech. Be sure they match up correctly.

4. If you are unsure of the meaning of a word, here are some strategies you can use:

- Use the process of elimination to narrow down the choices you know are wrong.
- Think about how you may have heard the word used before, and let context help you figure out its meaning.
- Think of words that share parts in common with the unknown word. For example, if *inconsequential* was unfamiliar to you, maybe you could recognize that it sounds like it has the word *consequence* in it. Combine that with the prefix *in-* (meaning "not" or "without"), and you get "without consequence," which puts you well on your way to figuring out that *inconsequential* means unimportant.

# Chapter 4: Spatial Ability

Spatial Ability is the second subtest on the CFAT. You will have 10 minutes to answer 15 questions. This test assesses your ability to visualize how 3-D objects are put together and how objects will look when manipulated.

## Spatial Ability Question Types

Spatial Ability questions are entirely visual; there are no words. The question prompt will be an image, and the answer choices will be four other images. These questions come in two basic types: put-together and take-apart.

## Put-Together Questions

In a put-together question, you will be shown an image of a flat pattern that could be folded to make a 3-D object. The answer choices will be four 3-D objects (or "forms"). You will need to select the object that matches what the pattern would look like when assembled.

In some of these questions, the answer choices will all be different three-dimensional shapes, and only one will fit the pattern. For these, carefully count the shapes that comprise the pattern and check to see which answer choice matches. Let's look at an example..

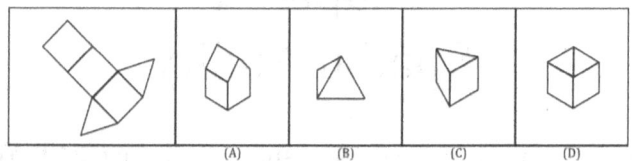

In this question, the pattern shows three squares and two triangles. Choice (A) includes a pentagon, so that cannot be the correct answer. Choice (B) has two visible triangles, but to make that pyramid shape, there must be additional triangles as the unseen faces, so this cannot be correct. Choice (C) shows two visible squares and one visible triangle. There must be an additional square attached to the third edge of the triangle, and the bottom of the figure must also be a triangle. So, with a total of three squares and two triangles, this matches our pattern. Let's check choice (D) just to be sure. Choice (D) shows two squares, each with a triangle on top. There must be additional unseen squares to complete the figure, which means there would also be additional triangles. This would give us more than the two triangles in the pattern, so choice (D) cannot be correct. The correct answer is (C).

Other put-together questions will show you four of the same figure, but the faces will have different designs on them. You'll have to figure out how the designs on the pattern would look when folded into the 3-D form. Here's an example.

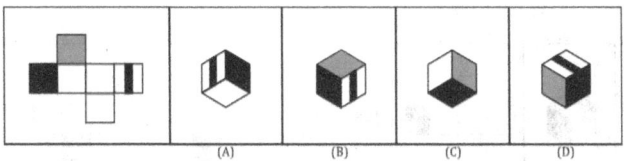

Here, all of the answer choices are cubes, so looking at the shapes won't help. We need to focus on the design. Let's take each choice in order. In choice (A), the stripe is vertical and white is on the bottom. Looking at the pattern, that means that the bottommost white square has become the bottom. The black square would wrap around to end up on the right of the striped square. This matches choice (A), so this is the correct answer. Let's look at why the other choices are incorrect. Choice (B) also shows the stripe as vertical, and the grey square is on top, meaning the same white square as in Choice (A) would have to be on the bottom. This time, however, the black square is shown to the left of the stripe, whereas it should be on the right, so this is incorrect. In choice (C), the black square is the bottom. If the pattern were folded so that grey was on the right side, the left side would be the stripe, not white, so this is incorrect. Choice (D) is incorrect because the grey side would not be visible if the stripe were on top in that orientation.

## Take-Apart Questions

A take-apart question is the reverse. You will be shown a 3-D object, and the four answer choices will be flat patterns. You must select the pattern that could be folded to create the 3-D object–what the object would look like if it were taken apart. Let's look at an example.

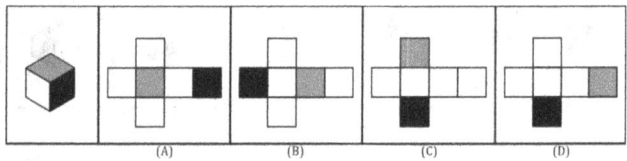

Here, the form is a cube, and all of the answer choices are the same pattern but with different colour patterns. Like in the put-together questions, go through each answer choice to see if it matches. Since all of the patterns have multiple white squares but only one each of the black and grey squares, you'll want to focus most on the positions of the black and grey. The form shows the black and grey touching each other. In choices (A), (B), and (C), the black and grey squares are positioned such that they could never touch each other on the folded cube. They would be on opposite sides. Only choice (D) would allow the black and grey to touch, so this is the correct answer.

# Chapter 5: Problem Solving

The final subtest on the CFAT is Problem Solving. You will have 45 minutes to answer 30 questions. These are mostly math-based, with some logical reasoning questions. You are strictly not allowed to use a calculator or any other device on the test, so all calculations must be performed by hand on the paper provided.

This chapter will review the basic mathematics concepts you are most likely to encounter on the CFAT.

## Arithmetic Operations

There are four basic operations in math–addition, subtraction, multiplication, and division.

***Addition*** is combining two or more numbers (called ***addends***) to find a total (called the ***sum***). For example, in the equation $4 + 1 = 5$, the addends 4 and 1 combine to create a sum of 5. In addition, the order of the addends does not actually matter. So, if you switched the addends in the previous example, you would still get the same sum: $1 + 4 = 5$.

***Subtraction*** is taking away an amount from a number to find the ***difference***. For example, $4 - 1 =$

3. Unlike with addition, the order in a subtraction problem matters. Switching the numbers would change the difference. For instance, changing the order in the previous example would give $1 - 4 = -3$.

***Multiplication*** is the repeated addition of equal groups (called ***factors***) to find the total (called the ***product***). For example, in the equation $2 \times 3 = 6$, the factors 2 and 3 multiply to equal the product, 6. Just like in addition, the order does not matter in multiplication, so $2 \times 3 = 6$ is the same as $3 \times 2 = 6$. In addition to the $\times$ symbol, there are other ways that multiplication can be indicated in an equation. If a number is directly in front of a set of parentheses, the number in front should be multiplied by whatever is inside the parentheses. For example, 3(2) indicates that you should multiply: $3 \times 2 = 6$. Also, if a number is attached to a variable (a letter representing an unknown value) with no operation sign in between, this indicates multiplication. So $2n$ is the same as saying $2 \times n$.

- The ***distributive property*** can be helpful in many problems involving multiplication. It states that when a number is in front of parentheses that contain operations, you can multiply the number in front by each number within the parentheses separately, then add the results to find the total. Here's an example of what the distributive property looks like.

$$a(b + c) = ab + ac$$

$$3(5 - 2) = (3 \times 5) + (3 \times -2)$$
$$3(3) = 15 + (-6)$$
$$9 = 9$$

**Division** is splitting a number (called the **dividend**) into an equal number of groups (called the **divisor**). The result (called the **quotient**) shows the number in each group. For example, $10 \div 2 = 5$ means that splitting 10 into 2 equal groups would result in 2 groups of 5 each.

If a number does not divide evenly, the quotient will not be an integer. Rather, it will include a fraction, decimal, or **remainder** (the integers left over after making as many equal groups as possible. For example, $7 \div 2$ does not come out evenly. The answer could be expressed as $3\frac{1}{2}$, 3.5, or $3R1$ (3 remainder 1).

## Special Cases

When performing arithmetic operations, it is important to remember some special cases. The first is performing operations with negative numbers. Here are the rules:
- Adding a negative number gives you the same answer as subtracting its positive counterpart. For example, $2 + (-3)$ is the same as $2 - 3 = -1$.
- Subtracting a negative number is just the same as adding its positive counterpart (a double negative makes a positive). For example, $2 - (-3) = 2 + 3 = 5$.

- Multiplication or division where one number is positive and the other is negative always yields a negative solution. For example, $10 \div -2 = -5$ and $2(-5) = 10$.
- Multiplication or division where both numbers have the same sign (whether positive or negative) always yields a positive solution. For example, $(-2)(-5) = 10$ and $2 \times 5 = 10$.

Multiplying and dividing with zero is also a special case.

- Any number multiplied by zero equals zero. For instance, $2 \times 0 = 0$.
- Zero divided by any number also equals zero. For example, $0 \div 2 = 0$.
- A number *cannot* be divided by zero. The result will be "undefined."

You may also occasionally encounter radicals on the CFAT. A ***radical*** is a number raised to a power, which means the number is multiplied by itself the given number of times. For example, $3^2 = 3 \times 3 = 9$, and $2^3 = 2 \times 2 \times 2 = 8$. Since you are not allowed a calculator on the CFAT, you will not encounter large or complicated radicals. You should simply know that it indicates repeated multiplication.

## Order of Operations

When solving an equation that includes more than one operation, following the correct order of operations is important. The acronym BEMDAS can help you remember the order: **Brackets**, **Exponents**,

Multiplication/Division (from left to right), and Addition/Subtraction (from left to right). Let's look at an example.

$$3(2 - 4) + 2^2 - 12 \div 3 =$$

**B**rackets $\quad 3(-2) + 2^2 - 12 \div 3 =$
**E**xponents $\quad 3(-2) + 4 - 12 \div 3 =$
**M**ultiplication/**D**ivision $\quad -6 + 4 - 4 =$
**A**ddition/**S**ubtraction $\quad -6$

# Fractions and Decimals

Some numbers contain partial integers. These can be expressed as either fractions or decimals. The CFAT frequently includes questions that require you to work with fractions and decimals, so you will want to be comfortable converting between them and performing operations with them.

## Fractions

A *fraction* is composed of two numbers separated by a horizontal bar. The number on top is called the **numerator**, representing a part. The bottom, or lower number is called the **denominator**, and it represents the whole. For example, two parts out of a total of three can be written as $\frac{2}{3}$.

Fractions that are equal in value (representing the same portion of a whole) are called **equivalent fractions**. Imagine a whole pizza. If you sliced the pizza into four equal pieces, each piece would be $\frac{1}{4}$ of the whole pizza. If you took that same pizza and cut it into eight equal slices instead, each of those slices would be $\frac{1}{8}$ of the whole. How many of these slices would you need to have the same amount of pizza as you did when each slice was $\frac{1}{4}$ of the pizza? You would need two. So, $\frac{2}{8} = \frac{1}{4}$. These are equivalent fractions, which represent the same portion of the whole. To find equivalent fractions, multiply both the numerator (upper) and the denominator (lower) of the fraction by the same number. In the pizza example above, $\frac{1}{4}$ was multiplied by 2 on the top and the bottom to give us $\frac{1}{4} = \frac{(1 \times 2)}{(4 \times 2)} = \frac{2}{8}$.

A specific type of equivalent fraction is called **lowest terms**. This means finding an equivalent fraction where both the numerator and the denominator are as small as possible. You do this by dividing both the top and the bottom by the same common factor. For example, in the fraction $\frac{10}{15}$, both the numerator (10) and the denominator (15) are divisible by 5. Dividing both the top and bottom by 5 will give us a reduced fraction: $\frac{10}{15} = \frac{(10 \div 5)}{(15 \div 5)} = \frac{3}{5}$. When a fraction has a numerator and denominator that no longer have any factors in common and cannot be reduced further, it is said to be in lowest terms.

## Operations with Fractions

It is important that you know the rules for performing arithmetic operations on fractions, as you will often be asked to do this on the CFAT.

For addition and subtraction of fractions, the most important rule is that the fractions must both have the same denominator (called a **common denominator**). If they have the same denominator, simply add or subtract the numerators of the fractions and keep the denominator the same. For example, $\frac{3}{11} + \frac{2}{11} = \frac{5}{11}$.

If the fractions have different denominators, you must first change one or both into equivalent fractions so that the denominators match. For example, say you need to add $\frac{1}{3}$ and $\frac{1}{2}$. The denominators are different; therefore, this rule tells us we need to identify a common denominator before we can add them together. Start by finding the least (or lowest) common multiple of 3 and 2. The multiples of 3 are 3, 6, 9, etc., and the multiples of 2 are 2, 4, 6, etc. Therefore, the lowest multiple they have in common is 6, so let's make that the common denominator. Now, we need to change each fraction into an equivalent fraction, each with a denominator of 6. Let's start with $\frac{1}{3}$. To get the denominator from 3 to 6, we'll need to multiply by 2. So, multiplying the top and bottom both by 2 gives us an equivalent fraction: $\frac{1}{3} = \frac{(1 \times 2)}{(3 \times 2)} = \frac{2}{6}$. Now do the same thing with the other fraction. To get the denominator from 2 to 6, we'll need to multiply by 3, so $\frac{1}{2} = \frac{(1 \times 3)}{(2 \times 3)} = \frac{3}{6}$. Now that the fractions both have the same denominator, we can add them: $\frac{2}{6} + \frac{3}{6} = \frac{5}{6}$.

Unlike adding and subtracting, multiplying and dividing fractions do not require a common denominator. To multiply fractions, simply multiply across: numerator times numerator and denominator times denominator. For example, $\frac{2}{3} \times \frac{3}{4} = \frac{(2 \times 3)}{(3 \times 4)} = \frac{6}{12}$. Typically, you will be expected to put fractions in lowest terms, so in this case that would be $\frac{6}{12} = \frac{1}{2}$.

Dividing fractions is the same thing as multiplying by the second fraction. In the **reciprocal** of a fraction, the numerator and denominator simply switch places. For example, the reciprocal of $\frac{3}{4}$ is $\frac{4}{3}$. Here's an example of division with fractions: $\frac{1}{3} \div \frac{3}{4}$. First, change the second fraction into its reciprocal, $\frac{4}{3}$. Then, multiply. $\frac{1}{3} \times \frac{4}{3} = \frac{4}{9}$.

## Decimals

Another way to represent a partial integer is with a **decimal**. Numbers to the left-hand side of a decimal point are integers. Numbers to the right-hand side of the decimal point show the portion of the value that is less than one. Each place value to the right of the decimal point is like a fraction out of a multiple of ten (e.g., $\frac{1}{10}$ = 0.1). The place values after the decimal point (from left to right) are called tenths, hundredths, thousandths, and so on. For example, two tenths of a second is 0.2 seconds.

## Operations with Decimals

Perform operations with decimals just as you would integers with one caveat—be very careful of the placement of the decimal point. If you are adding or subtracting, it is helpful to perform the operation vertically so you can line up the decimal points. For example,

|   |   |   | 3 | . | 2 | 5 |
|---|---|---|---|---|---|---|
| + |   | 1 | 2 | . | 4 |   |
|   |   | 1 | 5 | . | 6 | 5 |

For multiplication, one way to keep track of the correct decimal placement is to multiply the numbers as if they have no decimals, then add a decimal point into the answer at the end. The answer will have the same number of decimal places as both of the factors combined. For example, if you are multiplying 2.16 × 3.4, you can multiply 216 by 34 to get 7344. Then, look at the decimals. 2.16 has two numbers after the decimal, and 3.4 has one, so the answer needs 2 + 1 = 3 decimal places. That means the answer should be 7.344.

With division, it is often easiest to get rid of the decimals by multiplying both the dividend and the divisor by whatever multiple of 10 is needed to create an integer. Take, for example, 3 ÷ 0.5. To get rid of the decimal in 0.5, you would need to multiply by 10. You can do this can get the same answer as long as you also multiply the 3 by 10. So, 3 ÷ 0.5 becomes 30 ÷ 5 = 6.

## Converting Between Fractions and Decimals

Some questions may require you to convert between fractions and decimals. Converting a fraction to a decimal is simple. Take the decimal point out of the number; this will be your numerator. The denominator will be a multiple of 10 that has the same number of zeroes as there are place values to the right of the decimal point in the original number. Let's take 0.26, for example. The numerator will be 26. The original number had two decimal places, so the denominator will have two zeroes: 100. That means $0.26 = \frac{26}{100}$. Reduced to lowest terms, this is equal to $\frac{13}{50}$.

To convert a fraction into its decimal, there are two main methods you can use. The first is to simply divide the numerator by the denominator. For example, $\frac{3}{4} = 3 \div 4 = 0.75$. Remember, you aren't allowed to use a calculator on the CFAT, however, so sometimes long division might be tricky or time-consuming. A second method is to convert the fraction to an equivalent fraction whose denominator is a multiple of 10, then put the numerator after the decimal point. Let's use $\frac{3}{4}$ as our example again. The lowest multiple of 10 that 4 goes into evenly is 100, so we'll make that the denominator as we create an equivalent fraction: $\frac{3}{4} = \frac{(3 \times 25)}{(4 \times 25)} = \frac{75}{100}$. Putting the 75 to the right of the decimal gives 0.75.

## Algebraic Equations

Algebra on the CFAT is very minimal; however, basic familiarity with variables and how to solve a simple algebraic equation can help you solve many types of problems.

**Variables** are letters used to represent unknown values in an equation. The most commonly-used variable is $x$, but a variable can be any letter. A number attached in front of a variable is called a **coefficient**. So, in the case of $3x$, 3 is the coefficient, and $x$ is the variable. The fact that they are attached with no sign in between implies multiplication.

An algebraic equation is one that includes a variable. When solving an algebraic equation, your goal is to isolate the variable (get it alone on one side of the equals sign). When you do, you'll know the variable's value (e.g., $x = 3$). When solving an algebraic equation, you must follow one simple but important rule: whatever operations you perform to one side of the equals sign, you must do to the other. So, if you add 4 to the left side of an equation, you must also add 4 to the right side. Let's try an example.

$$10x - 4 = 7x + 8$$
$$\phantom{10x}-7x \phantom{-4=}-7x$$
$$3x - 4 = 8$$
$$\phantom{3x}+4 \phantom{-=}+4$$

$$3x = 12$$
$$\div 3 \quad \div 3$$
$$x = 4$$

## Algebra in Word Problems

Algebra can be useful for solving word problems. When you have an unknown number, represent it with a variable and use the information given in the question to create an equation to solve.

> **Example:**
> *Rachel is 4 years older than Jesse. Two years from now, Rachel will be twice as old as Jesse is now. How old is Rachel now?*

Let the variable $r$ represent Rachel's age now. Since Rachel is 4 years older than Jesse, Jesse's age can be represented as $r - 4$. Two years from now, Rachel's age will be $r + 2$. We also know that in two years, Rachel will be twice as old as Jesse is now, so she will be $2(r - 4)$. Set these two expressions as equal to each other and solve to find Rachel's current age ($r$).

$$r + 2 = 2(r - 4)$$
$$r + 2 = 2r - 8$$
$$2 = r - 8$$
$$10 = r$$

So Rachel is currently 10 years old.

## Ratios, Proportions, and Percents

Many questions on the Problem Solving subtest are word problems involving ratios, proportions, rates, and percentages. Getting comfortable with these types of problems is very important to your CFAT success.

## Ratios

A **ratio** compares two or more values. In word problems, ratios often compare parts of a group. Say, for example, a family owns five pets–three cats and two dogs. The ratio of cats to dogs in the family is 3 to 2. Ratios can be expressed in words ("3 to 2"), as a fraction $\left(\frac{3}{2}\right)$, or with a colon (3:2). Ratios can also represent the relationship between the part and the whole. So the ratio of dogs to the total number of pets is 2:5.

The values in a ratio don't always represent the exact number of things being compared; rather, they show the relationship between them in lowest terms. For example, if the ratio of students to teachers is said to be 8 to 1, that could mean that there are 8 students and 1 teacher, but it *could* mean that there are 80 students and 10 teachers, or any other multiple. All you can say for sure is that for every 8 students in the group, there is 1 teacher. If you know the total number in the group, you can use the ratio to solve for the exact number in each group. For example, if the student-to-teacher ratio is 8:1 and there are a total of 45 people altogether, we can set up an equation to find out how many teachers and students there are.

$$8x + 1x = 45$$
$$9x = 45$$
$$x = 5$$

So, the number of students is $8x = 8(5) = 40$, and the number of teachers is $1x = 1(5) = 5$.

A ***rate*** is defined as a special type of ratio which expresses "something per something," such as "km per hour." Most rates appear in word problems related to distance, time, speed, or cost. In these problems, pay close attention to the units being used. Some questions may require you to convert between units. Another example of a rate is "$ per gram."

## Proportions

A ***proportion*** consists of two ratios set equal to each other. These problems are easiest to solve if you put the proportions in fraction form. That way, you can solve by cross-multiplying (multiplying the numerator of one fraction by the denominator of another, or vice versa, then setting the products equal to each other).

> **Example:**
> *On a map, the distance between two towns is 2.5 cm. The map's scale indicates that every cm on the map represents 8 km in real life. How far apart are these towns in real life?*

Solve using a proportion. We know that 1 cm represents 8 km, so our first ratio is $\frac{1}{8}$. The measured distance between the towns on the map is 2.5 cm. Let $x$ represent the unknown real-life distance between them (in km). So, the

second ratio is $\frac{2.5}{x}$. Set these equal to each other and cross-multiply to solve.
$$\frac{1}{8} = \frac{2.5}{x}$$
$$1x = 20$$
$$x = 20$$
The distance between the two towns is 20 km.

# Percents

A ***percent*** is a ratio out of 100. You can use a simple proportion to solve many percent questions:
$$\frac{\%}{100} = \frac{part}{whole}$$
For example, if you need to calculate 20% of 40, you can set up the proportion $\frac{20}{100} = \frac{x}{40}$. Cross-multiplying gives you $800 = 100x$, and dividing both sides by 100 yields $8 = x$.

Some CFAT questions may involve a ***percent change***, which tells how much change has occurred between an original value and a new value. This most often shows up on the exam in word problems involving sales. The formula for a percent change is $\frac{\%\ change}{100} = \frac{Amount\ of\ change}{Original\ value}$.

**Example:**
*A pair of jeans that normally sells for $45 is on sale for 15% off. What is the sale price of the jeans?*

Start by setting up a proportion using the percent change formula.
$$\frac{15}{100} = \frac{x}{45}$$
$$15(45) = 100x$$
$$675 = 100x$$
$$6.75 = x$$

So, the jeans are on sale for $6.75 less than normal. Be careful, though. This is the discount amount, and the question asks for the sale price, so you're not done. Subtract the amount of discount from the original price to find the actual sale price. $45 − $6.75 = $38.25. (Note: On the CFAT, $6.75 would probably be listed as one of the wrong answer choices. This is why it is imperative to carefully check that you have found the value the question is asking for.)

Sometimes, you may need to convert between percentages and decimals. Since a percent is out of 100, it can be written as a number with two decimal places. For example, 25% is equal to 0.25.

A specific type of percent problem involves simple *interest*. For instance, a question might ask how much interest a loan would accrue after a given number of years at a certain interest rate. For these questions, use the formula $I = Prt$, where $I$ is the dollar amount of the interest, $P$ is the principal (the amount of money you started with), $r$ is the annual interest rate (the percentage, expressed as a decimal), and $t$ is the time in years.

**Example:**
*Chad takes out a $1,000 loan at an interest rate of 5% per year. At the end of 3 years, how much will Chad owe in total?*

Plug the given values into the interest formula.
$$I = Prt$$
$$I = 1,000(0.05)(3)$$
$$I = 150$$

The interest is $150, so at the end of 3 years, Chad will owe $1,000 + $150 = $1,500.

# Statistics

The CFAT may ask word problems involving basic principles of statistics and probability.

## Averages

The **average** of a set of numbers (also called the **mean**) is found by adding up the terms and dividing by the number of terms. For example, let's find the average of 15, 18, and 24.

$$Average = \frac{Sum\ of\ terms}{Number\ of\ terms}$$
$$Average = \frac{15 + 18 + 24}{3}$$
$$Mean = \frac{57}{3}$$
$$Mean = 19$$

## Probability

**Probability** is the statistical likelihood that an event will occur. Basic probability can be expressed as a ratio between the number of desired outcomes and the total number of possible outcomes.

$$Probability = \frac{number\ of\ desired\ outcomes}{number\ of\ possible\ outcomes}$$

For example, let's calculate the probability of rolling an even number on a standard six-sided die. The even numbers on a die are 2, 4, and 6, so there are 3 ways to get a desired outcome. There are 6 possible numbers you could roll in total. Therefore, the probability of rolling an even number would be $\frac{3}{6}$, which reduces to $\frac{1}{2}$.

# Geometry

The Problem Solving subtest may include some geometry questions. You should be familiar with the basic characteristics of common two-dimensional shapes, along with the concepts of area and volume. You may also see logical reasoning questions involving geometric figures.

## Two-Dimensional Shapes

A **shape** is a closed figure. On the CFAT, you will primarily deal with three types of shapes: triangles, quadrilaterals, and circles.

- **Triangles** have three straight sides.
- **Quadrilaterals** have four straight sides. There are several types of quadrilaterals. The ones you will see most frequently on the CFAT are rectangles and squares. A **rectangle**

always has four right angles and two pairs of equal sides. A ***square*** is a unique type of rectangle where all of its four sides are the same length.
- ***Circles*** have no straight sides. They are perfectly round and contain a total of 360°. The point precisely in the middle of the circle is called the ***centre***. On the other hand, the distance from the centre to any point on the circle is called the ***radius*** ($r$). The distance all the way across the circle, passing through the middle, or centre, is called the ***diameter*** ($d$). Finally, the diameter is twice as long as the radius.

Questions about shapes often deal with ***perimeter***, or the distance around the shape. For any straight-sided shape (called a ***polygon***), you find the perimeter by adding the individual lengths of all the sides. The perimeter of a circle is known as the ***circumference***, and it can be calculated using the formula $C = \pi d$ or $C = 2\pi r$. On CFAT questions involving circles, they tell you to use the approximate value of $\pi$ in its place, which is 3.14. The question will indicate whether you should give an answer in terms of $\pi$ or substitute 3.14.

Other shape questions ask about ***area***, which is the total space inside a shape. Here's how to find the area of each shape you may encounter on the CFAT.
- Rectangles: $Area = length \times width$

- Squares: The rectangle formula still works, but since the length and width remain the same in a square, you can also say $Area = side^2$.
- Triangles: $Area = \frac{1}{2} base \times height$, where the base is one side of the triangle and the height is the perpendicular distance from the base to the opposite corner of the triangle.

## Three-Dimensional Figures

***Three-dimensional figures*** are solid forms with depth. The flat sides of a three-dimensional figure are called ***faces***. The places where the faces join together are called ***edges***.

Here are the most common three-dimensional figures.
- **Rectangular prism:** six rectangular faces and all angles measure 90°; opposite faces are identical
- **Cube:** a type of rectangular prism where the faces are all identical squares
- **Pyramid:** one base that can be a triangle, square, or rectangle; the other faces are triangles that meet at a single point
- **Cone:** one circular base and one point
- **Cylinder:** two circular bases (looks like a tube)
- **Sphere:** perfectly round with no edges or faces (looks like a ball)

The two measurements you should be familiar with for three-dimensional figures are surface area and volume.

***Surface area*** is the total area on the outer surface of the figure. For any figure with all flat faces, you simply find the area of each face and add them together. For example, for a pyramid, you would find the area of the base and add that to the areas of each of the triangular sides. For a cube, you can just find the area of one face and multiply that by six, since all of the faces of a cube are identical. On the CFAT, you will not be asked to calculate the surface area of figures with curved surfaces rather than flat faces (such as spheres, cylinders, and cones) since these processes are more complex.

***Volume*** is defined as the space inside a three-dimensional object. You must know how to calculate the volume of a rectangular prism ($V = lwh$) and a cube ($V = s^3$). If you are asked to calculate the volume of another figure, such as a cylinder, you will be provided with the formula.

# Logical Reasoning

Some questions on the CFAT ask you to apply logical reasoning to find a pattern or relationship among numbers, words, or images. Most commonly, these questions take the form of sequences and analogies.

## Sequences

A ***sequence*** is a list of items that follow a pattern or rule. For example, the sequence 2, 4, 6, 8, 10... is comprised of even numbers. On the Problem Solving subtest, you may be asked to identify a number missing from a sequence or predict the next number in a sequence. In either case, you must analyze the numbers to find the rule, then apply the rule to find the missing value.

Here are the most common types of sequences you are likely to encounter.
- Arithmetic Sequence: Each term is found by adding or subtracting a value from the previous term. For example, in the sequence 3, 7, 11, 15..., each term is found by adding 4 to the previous term, so the next term would be 19.
- Geometric Sequence: Each term is calculated by multiplying the previous term by the same value. For example, in the sequence −3, 6, −12, 24..., each term is found by multiplying the previous term by −2, so the next term would be −48.
- Multi-step Sequence: Multiple operations are used to get from one term to the next. For example, in the sequence 2, 5, 11, 23..., the rule is $2n + 1$. You multiply a term by 2 and then add 1 to find the next term. In this case, the next term would be 47.

## Analogies

Analogies on the Problem Solving subtest are often image-based. Just as in verbal analogies, you will use the relationship between one pair of figures to complete a second pair (for more on analogies, refer to Chapter 3).

## Example:

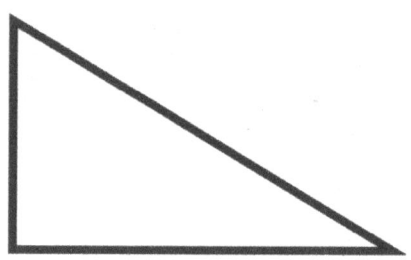

1. 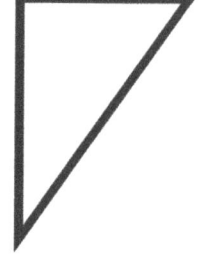 is to

as

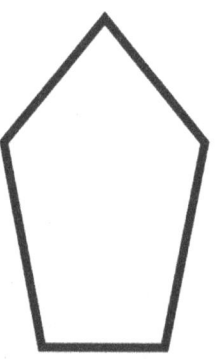

is to

THE CFAT STUDY GUIDE

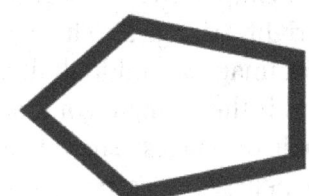

A.

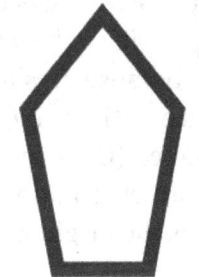

B.

C.

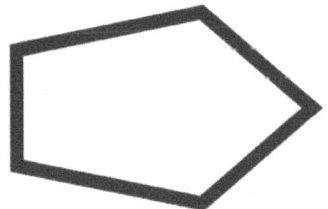

D.

First, determine the relationship between the first two images. They are both right triangles. The second image shows what the first image would look like if it were rotated clockwise and if the triangle got smaller. Now look at the second pair of images. The one given in the question stem is a pentagon. To complete the analogy, we will need a pentagon that is smaller than the original and that has been rotated clockwise. Choice (D) fits this description, so it is the correct answer. Choice (A) is incorrect because it shows a counterclockwise rotation. Choice (B) is incorrect because it shows no rotation. Choice (C) is incorrect because while it shows the correct rotation, the pentagon shown is the same size as the original rather than smaller.

# Chapter 6: Personality Inventory

After you complete the CFAT, you will be given a personality inventory. **It does not count toward your CFAT score**, but it is another factor recruiters will use to evaluate your candidacy. This computer-based, 30-minute assessment is designed to give recruiters more information about your personal characteristics. This helps them determine whether or not you are likely to be well-suited for the positions in which you are interested.

The personality inventory is adaptive, which means the test adjusts based on how you answer the questions. This allows the evaluators to get a more nuanced understanding of your personality. Examples of things the survey may ask you about are time management, your work preferences, how you handle stress, your communication style, how you work with others, how you handle disagreement, and how you would likely respond in a given scenario.

There is no way to study for this test, so try to go into it with a clear head. Answer the questions honestly and instinctually–go with your gut and don't overthink it. Don't try to guess how the recruiters want you to answer; instead, be forthcoming in your responses. Ensuring that your personality is a good fit for your chosen career path is not only in the CAF's best interest, but yours as well. Ultimately, you are more likely to be satisfied and successful in a position that is a good match for you.

# Chapter 7: Practice Test 1

In this chapter, you will find **three full-length practice tests**, each with 60 questions. We recommend you time yourself while taking each section to simulate actual testing conditions. The answers and explanations for these practice tests are found in Chapter 8.

## Practice Test 1
### Verbal Skills
**Number of questions: 15**
**Time: 5 minutes**

*Directions: This section tests your understanding of words. Each question has four answer choices. Select the one that best answers the question.*

9. INQUIRE means the same as
    A. answer
    B. peddle
    C. ignore
    D. investigate

10. BARTER means the same as
    A. trade
    B. return

C. hoard
  D. bequeath

11. FREEZING is to COOL as INFURIATING is to
    A. frigid
    B. irksome
    C. anger
    D. pleasant

12. WITHER means the same as
    A. shrivel
    B. grow
    C. moisten
    D. brighten

13. LENIENT is the opposite of
    A. relaxed
    B. intelligent
    C. strict
    D. deceitful

14. SATISFIED means the same as
    A. content
    B. unhappy
    C. lazy
    D. ecstatic

15. IGUANA is to REPTILE as SHEEP is to
    A. goat
    B. mammal
    C. animal
    D. lizard

16. STATELY means the same as
    A. nonchalant
    B. small
    C. dignified
    D. aggressive

17. SIGHT is to EYESORE as SOUND is to
    A. cacophony
    B. melody
    C. instrument
    D. voice

18. PLACATE means the same as
    A. prepare
    B. entertain
    C. inspire
    D. pacify

19. To SUBSTANTIATE a claim means to
    A. disprove
    B. confirm
    C. undermine
    D. argue

20. DECREE means the same as
    A. suggestion
    B. increment
    C. question
    D. proclamation

21. TRICKLE is to DELUGE as BREEZE is to
    A. flood

B. gale
C. tornado
D. rain

22. PERCEIVE means the same as
    A. obtain
    B. avoid
    C. notice
    D. create

23. Someone who DITHERS is
    A. hasty
    B. indecisive
    C. confident
    D. enthusiastic

# Spatial Ability
**Number of questions: 15**
**Time: 10 minutes**

***Directions:*** *This section tests your ability to recognize the relationship between a form and its pattern. For each question, you will see a row of five pictures. If the first image on the left shows a PATTERN, you must choose which FORM (A, B, C, or D) could be created by folding the given pattern. If the first image on the left shows a FORM, you must choose which PATTERN (A, B, C, or D) would be needed to create that form.*

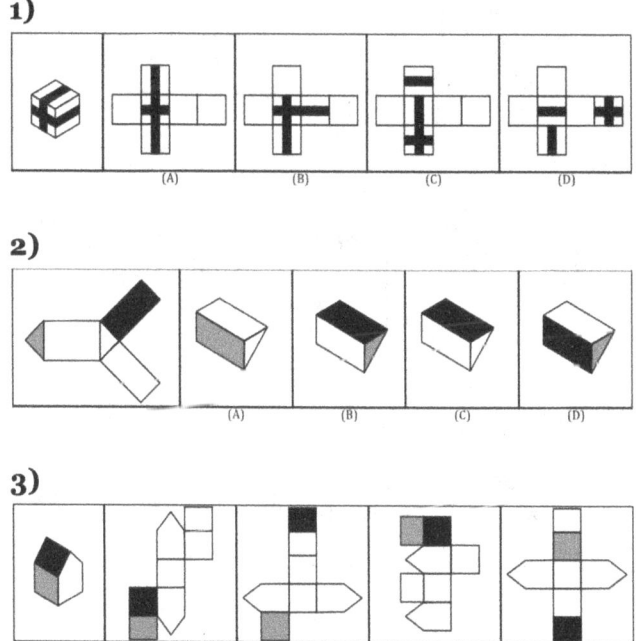

1)

2)

3)

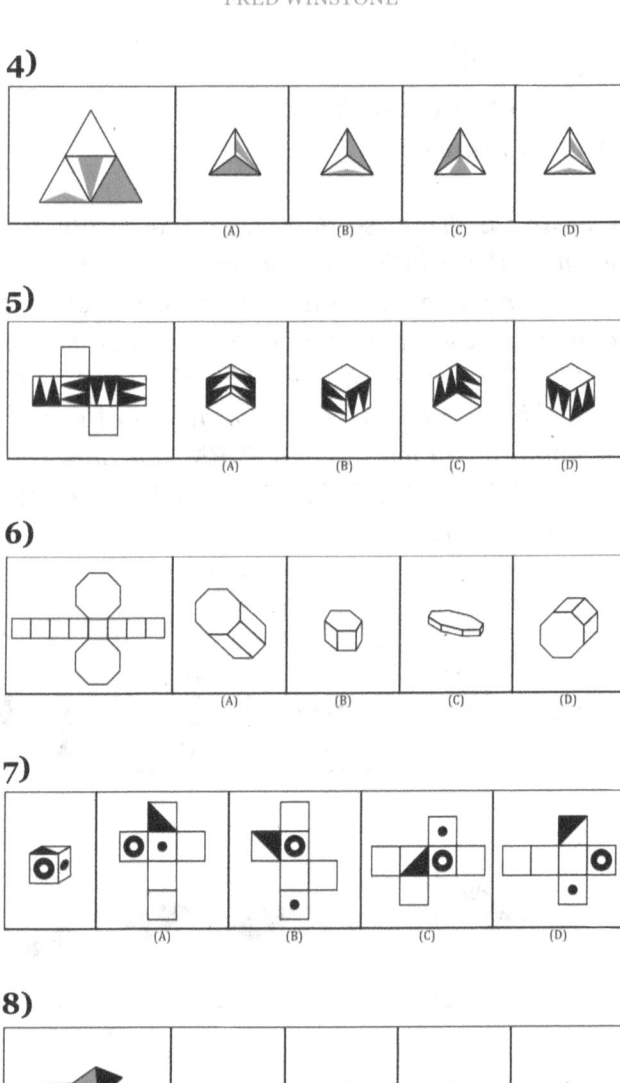

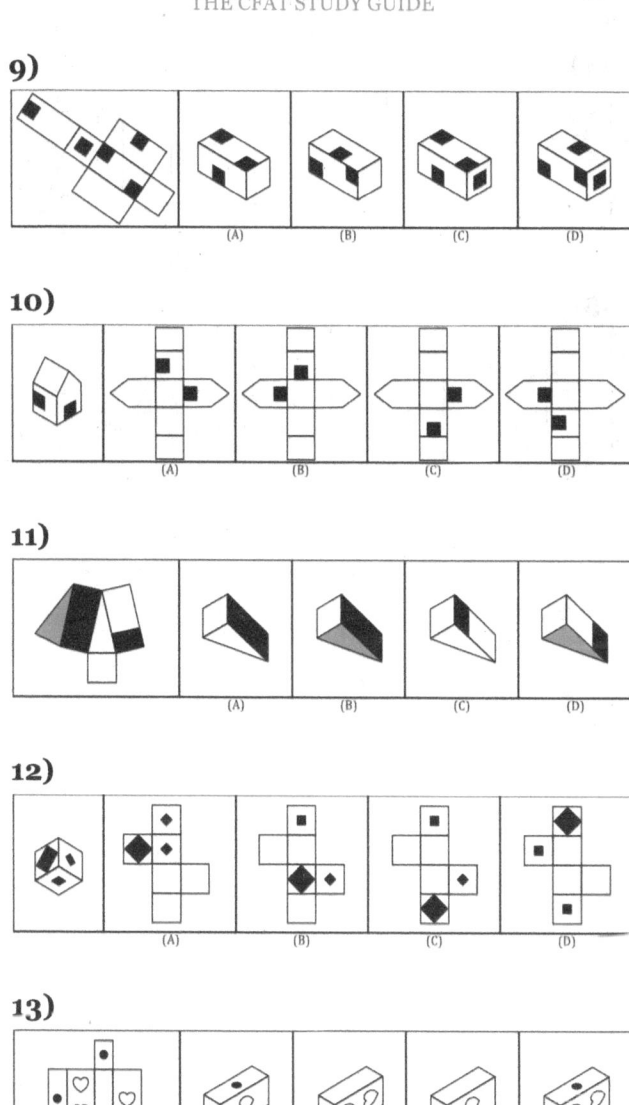

**14)**

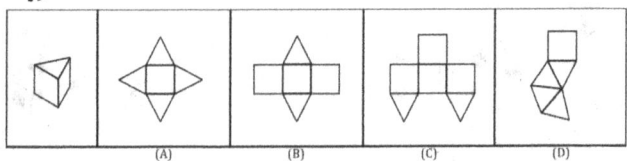

**15)**

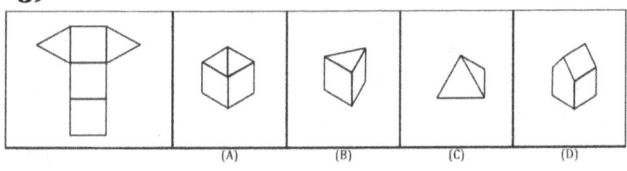

# Problem Solving
**Number of questions: 30**
**Time: 45 minutes**

*Directions: This section tests your ability to solve problems. Each question has four answer choices. Select the one that best answers the question.*

1. If a car travels on a road at an average speed of 84 kilometres per hour, how far will the car travel in 25 minutes?
    A. 4 km
    B. 18 km
    C. 26 km
    D. 35 km

2. Daniel and Maya both arrived at work at exactly 8:00 yesterday. Daniel left his house at 7:42, but it took Daniel twice as long to get to work as it took Maya. Assuming it takes her the same amount of time to get to work each day, what time will Maya arrive at work tomorrow if she leaves her house at 7:49?
    A. 7:51
    B. 7:58
    C. 8:00
    D. 8:07

3. A certain type of army battalion consists of five companies, each of which contains three

platoons. How many platoons are in two such battalions?

    A. 10
    B. 15
    C. 16
    D. 30

4. 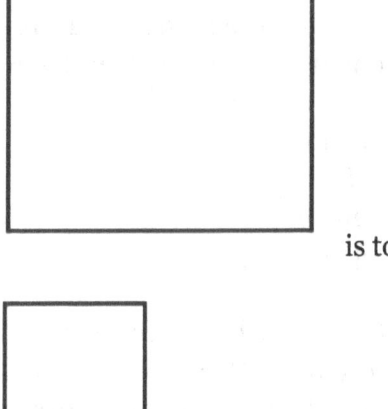 is to

as

THE CFAT STUDY GUIDE

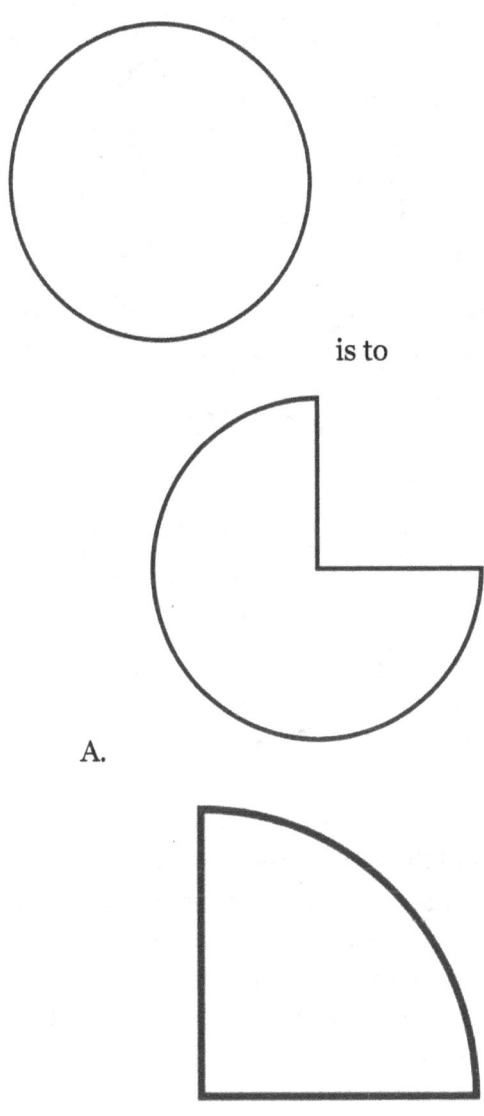

is to

A.

B.

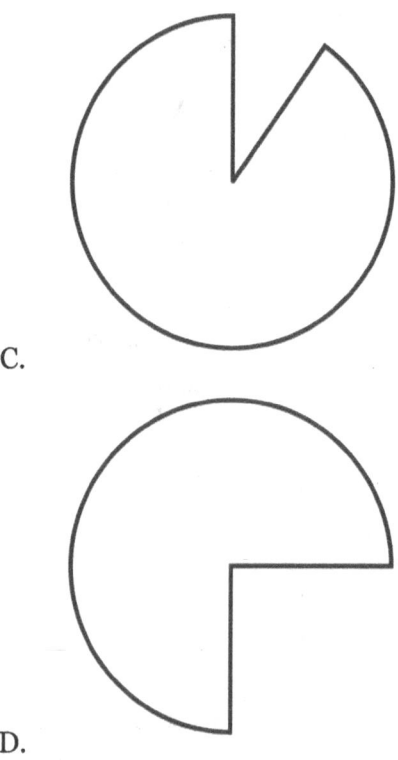

C.

D.

5. 64% of the students currently enrolled in a class are female, and the rest are male. If one male student were to drop out of the class, the males would make up exactly one-third of the class. How many students are currently in the class?
   A. 16
   B. 24
   C. 25
   D. 36

6. Which number comes next in the following sequence? 2, 6, 18, 54, ...
    A. 58
    B. 90
    C. 108
    D. 162

7. Three friends share a pizza and, between them, eat the entire pizza. Ben eats 50% more pizza than Alex, and Carlos eats the same amount of pizza as Ben. What portion of the pizza does Alex eat?
    A. $\frac{1}{5}$
    B. $\frac{1}{4}$
    C. $\frac{1}{3}$
    D. $\frac{1}{2}$

8. What is $\frac{1}{5}$ divided by 0.3?
    A. $\frac{3}{50}$
    B. $\frac{1}{15}$
    C. $\frac{3}{5}$
    D. $\frac{2}{3}$

9. Which of the following would be the next two shapes in the pattern below?

A.

B.

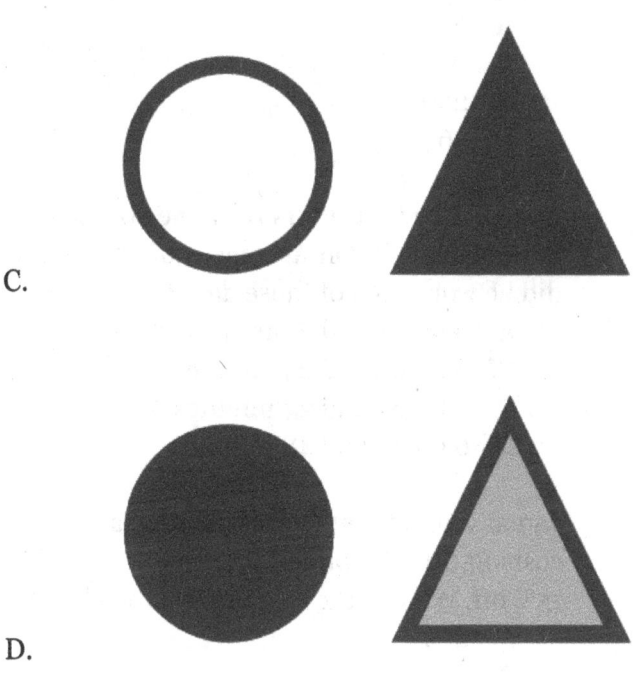

C.

D.

10. How many more multiples of 4 than multiples of 8 are there between 21 and 67?
    A. 5
    B. 6
    C. 11
    D. 17

11. Which of the following has the highest value?
    A. 0.4
    B. $\frac{3}{5}$
    C. 20% of 0.5
    D. $0.3^2$

12. Marcy works out five times each week. How many times does she work out each year?
    A. 60
    B. 190
    C. 260
    D. 365

13. Luke worked 34 hours over the course of five days last week. On average, how many hours did he work each of those days?
    A. 6 hours and 8 minutes
    B. 6 hours and 25 minutes
    C. 6 hours and 34 minutes
    D. 6 hours and 48 minutes

14. Jamal wants to buy a cell phone that normally costs $500. The phone is currently on sale for 15% off. What is the sale price of the phone?
    A. $75
    B. $375
    C. $425
    D. $485

15. Anna has a candlemaking business. She buys $300 worth of supplies. If each candle sells for $12, what is the minimum number of candles she must sell in order to make a profit?
    A. 24
    B. 25
    C. 26
    D. 27

16. In a survey of 50 households, 60% of the households owned a dog, a cat, or both. If 19 of the households surveyed owned a dog and 23 owned a cat, how many households owned both a dog and a cat?
    A. 8
    B. 12
    C. 15
    D. 19

17. What is the missing number in the following sequence?
    $$-1, 2, -4, ?, -16, 32$$
    A. −8
    B. −7
    C. 8
    D. 12

18. If 20% of a number is 45, what is the number?
    A. 9
    B. 65
    C. 225
    D. 900

19. A bag happens to contain 3 red marbles, 4 blue marbles, and 5 green marbles. What is the probability that a marble pulled from the bag will NOT be red?
    A. $\frac{1}{9}$
    B. $\frac{1}{4}$
    C. $\frac{1}{3}$
    D. $\frac{3}{4}$

20. Michelle is 16 years old. Jordan's age is four years less than twice Michelle's age. How old will Jordan be two years from now?
    A. 26
    B. 28
    C. 30
    D. 32

21. Brand A sells a box of eight granola bars for $2.72. Brand B sells a box of six granola bars for $2.28. Brand C sells a box of 16 granola bars for $5.12. Brand D sells a box of 12 granola bars for $3.36. Which brand has the lowest price per granola bar?
    A. Brand A
    B. Brand B
    C. Brand C
    D. Brand D

22. $\left(\frac{1}{5} \div \frac{3}{4}\right) - \left(\frac{3}{5} \div 6\right) = ?$
    A. $\frac{1}{15}$
    B. $\frac{1}{6}$
    C. $\frac{7}{30}$
    D. $\frac{19}{60}$

23. It takes the planet Mercury 59 days to complete one rotation on its axis, and it takes 88 days for Mercury to complete one orbit around the Sun. In the time it takes Mercury to orbit the Sun

three times, how many times will Mercury make a complete rotation on its axis?

    A. 4
    B. 9
    C. 27
    D. 87

24. $2^2 + (13 - 5) \times 3 = ?$

    A. 2
    B. 15
    C. 28
    D. 36

25. The area of a circle is expressed by the formula $A = 3.14r^2$, where $A$ is the area and $r$ is the radius. What is the radius of a circle whose area is 28.26 cm²?

    A. 2 cm
    B. 3 cm
    C. 4.5 cm
    D. 5.5 cm

26. Joyce takes out a $5,000 loan with a simple interest rate of 4% per year. If she pays back the loan in 3 years, how much will she have paid in total?

    A. $600
    B. $5,200
    C. $5,600
    D. $5,800

27. On a map, the cities of Toronto and Ottawa are 11.7 cm apart. In real life, the cities are approximately 351 km apart. If the real-life distance between Toronto and Kingston is approximately 243 km, how far apart will they be on the map?
   A. 7.5 cm
   B. 8.1 cm
   C. 9.4 cm
   D. 10.3 cm

28. Calculate the surface area of a box that is 15 cm long, 10 cm wide, and 6 cm high?
   A. 300 cm²
   B. 500 cm²
   C. 600 cm²
   D. 900 cm²

29. If 15% of a number is 27, what is $\frac{2}{3}$ of the same number?
   A. 90
   B. 120
   C. 180
   D. 270

30. Kathy can type 75 words per minute. If she begins typing at 9:25 and doesn't stop, at what time will she type her 1,000th word?
   A. 9:37
   B. 9:38
   C. 9:39
   D. 9:40

# Chapter 8: Practice Test 2

## Verbal Skills
**Number of questions: 15**
**Time: 5 minutes**

*Directions: This section tests your understanding of words. Each question has four answer choices. Select the one that best answers the question.*

1. OUTCOME means the same as
    A. origin
    B. exit
    C. purpose
    D. result

2. FORTUNATE is to LUCK as HAPLESS is to
    A. happiness
    B. calamity
    C. stability
    D. triumph

3. SKEPTICISM means the same as
    A. doubt
    B. decisiveness
    C. bitterness
    D. certainty

4. DEVISE means the same as
    A. destroy
    B. trick
    C. separate
    D. formulate

5. WORDS are to AUTHOR as NOTES are to
    A. performer
    B. article
    C. composer
    D. symphony

6. MOTIF means the same as
    A. reason
    B. disorder
    C. distraction
    D. pattern

7. ATROCIOUS is the opposite of
    A. outrageous
    B. wonderful
    C. terrible
    D. mundane

8. CRUCIAL means the same as
    A. necessary
    B. worthless
    C. detracting
    D. available

9. TENACIOUS means the same as
    A. fearful
    B. determined
    C. unreliable
    D. friendly

10. A DISTRAUGHT person is
    A. calm
    B. ambitious
    C. apathetic
    D. upset

11. HAPHAZARD means the same as
    A. perilous
    B. systematic
    C. random
    D. unsuccessful

12. CAR is to STEERING WHEEL as HORSE is to
    A. rider
    B. reins
    C. animal
    D. saddle

13. SCARCE means the same as
    A. rare
    B. afraid
    C. frequent
    D. useless

14. A TEDIOUS task is
    A. entertaining

B. demanding
   C. dull
   D. unpredictable

15. ARID means the same as
    A. spirited
    B. dry
    C. proud
    D. abundant

THE CFAT STUDY GUIDE

## Spatial Ability
**Number of questions: 15**
**Time: 10 minutes**

*Directions: This section tests your ability to recognize the relationship between a form and its pattern. For each question, you will see a row of five pictures. If the first image on the left shows a PATTERN, you must choose which FORM (A, B, C, or D) could be created by folding the given pattern. If the first image on the left shows a FORM, you must choose which PATTERN (A, B, C, or D) would be needed to create that form.*

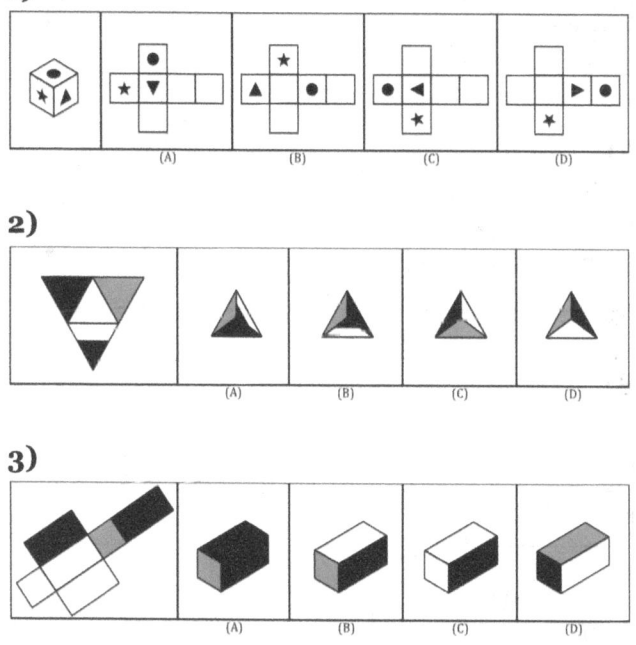

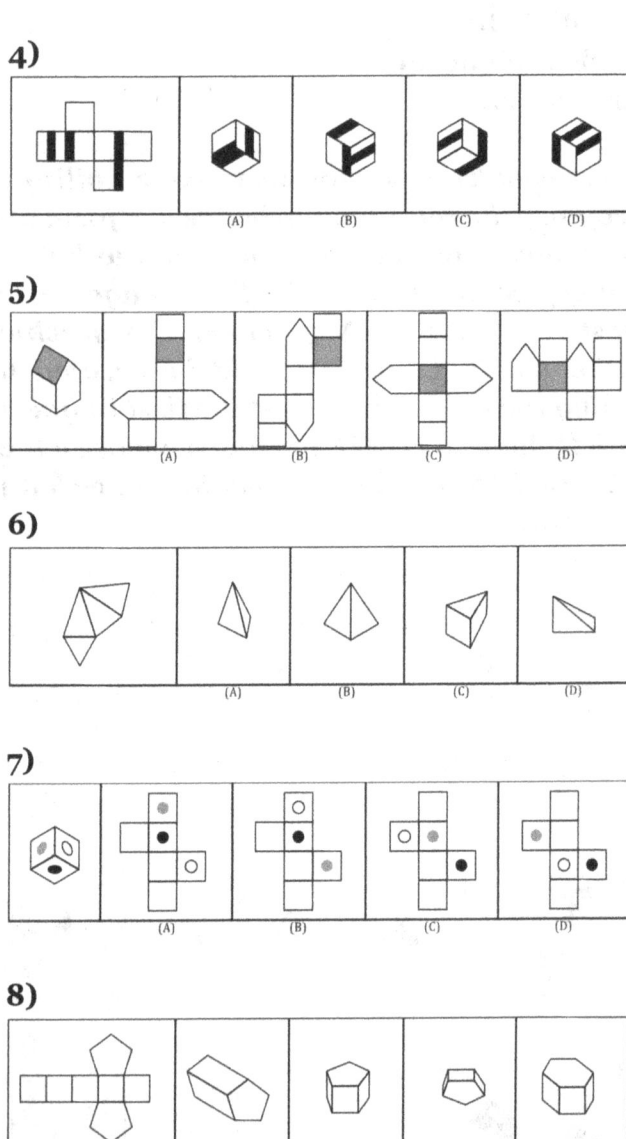

**9)**

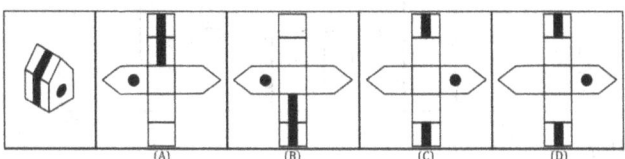

**10)**

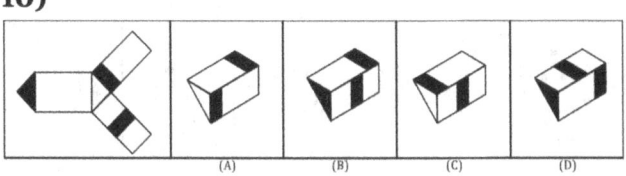

**11)**

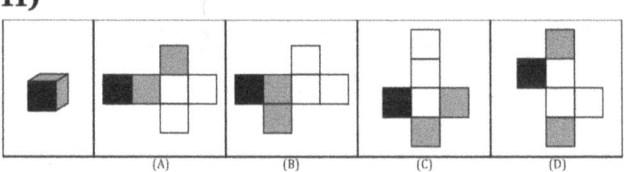

**12)**

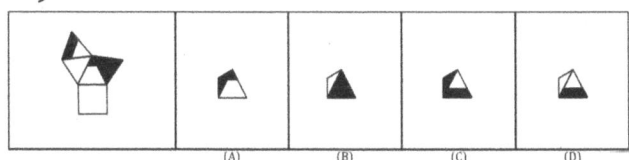

**13)**

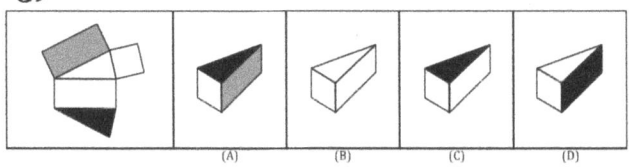

81

**14)**

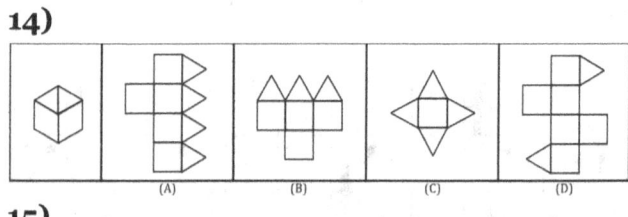

**15)**

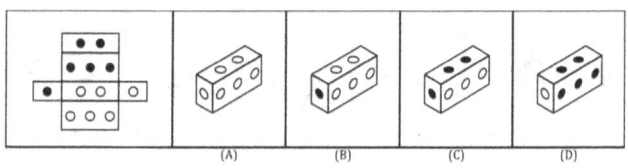

# Problem Solving
**Number of questions: 30**
**Time: 45 minutes**

*Directions: This section tests your ability to solve problems. Each question has four answer choices. Select the one that best answers the question.*

1. Rachel drove 45 km, and her vehicle's gasoline consumption averaged 8 L/100 km. If gasoline costs $1.20 per litre, how much did the gasoline for this trip cost?
    A. $3.00
    B. $3.60
    C. $4.32
    D. $6.75

2. The student-to-teacher ratio at a school is 18:1. Which of these could be the total number of students and teachers at the school?
    A. 324
    B. 378
    C. 418
    D. 450

3. How many seconds are there in one day?
    A. 1,440
    B. 3,600
    C. 10,080
    D. 86,400

4. When he receives his weekly paycheck, Craig deposits 20% of the money in a savings account. This week, he deposited $205.20. How much was his weekly paycheck?
   A. $225.20
   B. $1,026.00
   C. $1,231.20
   D. $4,104.00

5. If there are approximately 3.785 L in a gallon, how many mL are in a half-gallon (to the nearest mL)?
   A. 1,893
   B. 2,839
   C. 3,785
   D. 7,570

6. William has gotten an average score of 85 on his last three tests. If he scores a 97 on his next test, by how many points will his average test score increase?
   A. 3
   B. 6
   C. 9
   D. 12

7. Which number comes next in the following sequence? 1, 3, 7, 15, 31...
   A. 43
   B. 57
   C. 63
   D. 71

8. 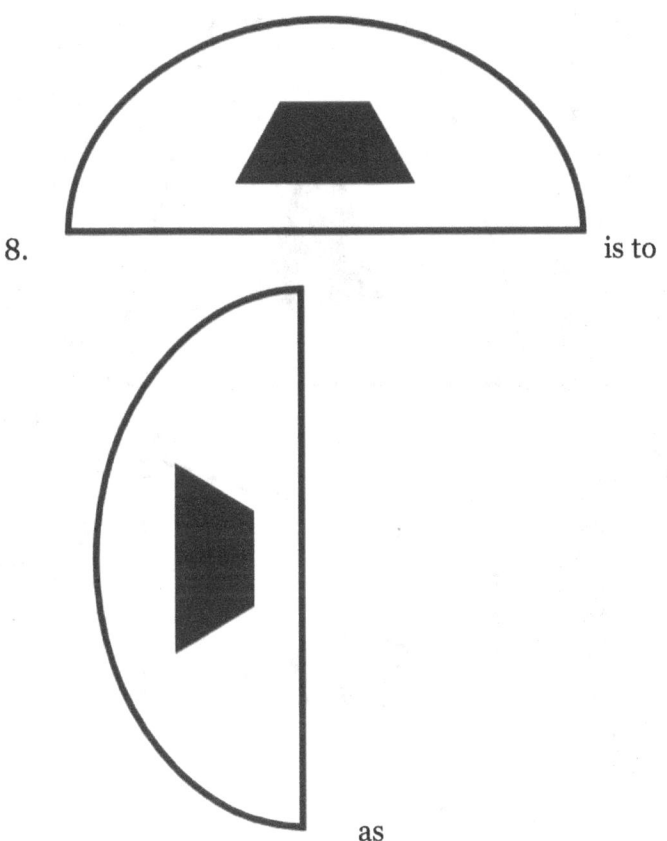 is to

as

is to

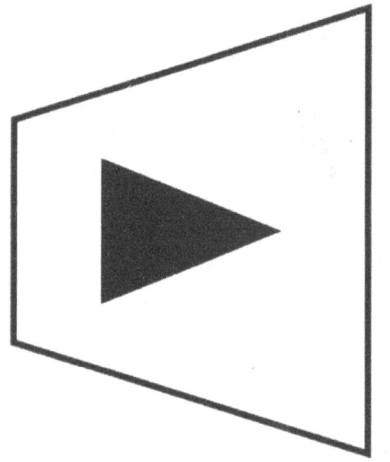

A.

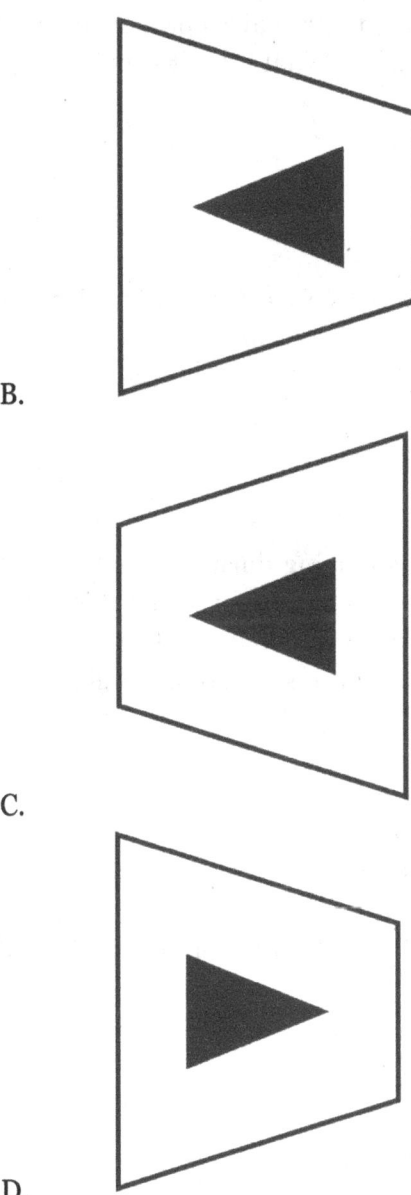

B.

C.

D.

9. Two positive integers have a product of 72 and a difference of 21. What is their sum?
    A. 17
    B. 18
    C. 27
    D. 34

10. What is the value of $2 \times 5^2 - (3 - 6) + (10 \div 2)$?
    A. 28
    B. 52
    C. 58
    D. 108

11. Kristin goes shopping during a storewide 25% off sale. She pays $41.70 for a pair of jeans and $21.00 for a shirt. How much more would Kristin have spent if she had paid full price for these items?
    A. $15.68
    B. $20.90
    C. $47.03
    D. $83.60

12. Which of the following numbers has the greatest value?
    A. 0.05
    B. $\frac{3}{50}$
    C. 4%
    D. $0.06^2$

13. After every 40 minutes of work, Hugo takes a 5-minute break. If Hugo starts working at 8:00 AM, how long will he have spent working by 11:00 AM?
    A. 2 hours
    B. 2 hours and 20 minutes
    C. 2 hours and 40 minutes
    D. 3 hours

14. Expressed as a decimal, $\frac{9}{36}$ is equal to
    A. 0.02
    B. 0.09
    C. 0.25
    D. 0.9

15. A certain three-digit number has digits that are all unique and sum to 10. What is the difference between the greatest and least possible values of this number?
    A. 136
    B. 462
    C. 774
    D. 910

16. In a group of 30 people, 14 speak French and 26 speak English. If everyone in the group speaks at least one of these languages, how many group members speak both French and English?
    A. 4
    B. 10
    C. 12
    D. 16

17. If the perimeter of a square was doubled, its area will increase by a factor of
    A. 2
    B. 4
    C. 6
    D. 8

18. A car travelling down a road at an average speed of 50 km per hour takes 2 hours to complete a trip. How much shorter would the trip have been if the car had instead travelled at an average speed of 60 km per hour?
    A. 20 minutes
    B. 40 minutes
    C. 1 hour and 20 minutes
    D. 1 hour and 40 minutes

19. In an office of 50 employees, 29 of them drive to work, 6% ride a bike to work, and the rest use public transportation to get to work. If one employee is randomly selected from this group, what is the probability that the employee gets to work using public transportation?
    A. $\frac{1}{6}$
    B. $\frac{3}{10}$
    C. $\frac{9}{25}$
    D. $\frac{9}{16}$

20. 80% of 60 is equal to 30% of what number?

A. 18
B. 40
C. 66
D. 160

21. A recipe for 12 cupcakes calls for $1\frac{1}{4}$ cups of flour. How many cups of flour would be needed to bake three dozen cupcakes?

    A. $2\frac{1}{2}$
    B. $2\frac{3}{4}$
    C. $3\frac{1}{2}$
    D. $3\frac{3}{4}$

22. When 5 is divided by 0.04, the quotient is

    A. 0.2
    B. 0.5
    C. 12.5
    D. 125

23. What is the average of $\frac{2}{5}$ and $\frac{4}{9}$?

    A. $\frac{2}{15}$
    B. $\frac{19}{45}$
    C. $\frac{3}{7}$
    D. $\frac{2}{3}$

24. At a cafe, Lisa pays $5.35 for a cup of coffee and a donut. Anita pays $6.95 for a cup of coffee and

two donuts. What would the price of three cups of coffee be?
- A. $4.80
- B. $6.15
- C. $11.25
- D. $12.30

25. $12 \times 3 - (-2) =$
- A. 12
- B. 32
- C. 38
- D. 60

26. Becky is 18 years old, which is two years more than half of Carl's age. Adam is two years older than Becky. How many years older than Adam is Carl?
- A. 12
- B. 14
- C. 20
- D. 32

27. Paul earns $45 per hour at his job. If he works for more than 40 hours in a given week, he earns overtime pay for those additional hours at a rate of 1.5 times his normal wage. How much would Paul earn if he worked 46 hours in a week?
- A. $1,935
- B. $2,070
- C. $2,205
- D. $3,105

28. Mei is packaging cupcakes at a bakery in boxes of six cupcakes. When she finishes filling the

boxes, she has no cupcakes left over. Which of these could NOT be the number of cupcakes she started with?

    A. 162
    B. 174
    C. 186
    D. 190

29. Troy wants to buy two books with list prices of $23.00 and $31.00. The bookstore is running a sale where if you buy one book at full price, you can buy a second book of equal or lesser value at 50% off. How much would Troy pay if he bought both books during the sale?

    A. $27.00
    B. $38.50
    C. $42.50
    D. $49.00

30. Which number comes next in the following sequence? 80, 20, 5...

    A. −10
    B. 1
    C. 1.25
    D. 2.5

# Chapter 9: Practice Test 3

## Verbal Skills
**Number of questions: 15**
**Time: 5 minutes**

*Directions: This section tests your understanding of words. Each question has four answer choices. Select the one that best answers the question.*

1. INDICATE means the same as
    A. explore
    B. ignore
    C. promote
    D. show

2. LIKE is to LOVE as DISLIKE is to
    A. mistrust
    B. abhor
    C. omit
    D. adore

3. CONSENSUS means the same as
    A. agreement
    B. dissension
    C. happiness
    D. uncertainty

4. HINDER means the same as
    A. allow
    B. aid
    C. regret
    D. prevent

5. OPEN is to CLOSE as BEGIN is to
    A. shut
    B. commence
    C. terminate
    D. unseal

6. MODIFY means the same as
    A. maintain
    B. calculate
    C. predict
    D. alter

7. PRECEDE is the opposite of
    A. predate
    B. follow
    C. exit
    D. undergo

8. OBVIOUS means the same as
    A. clear
    B. vague
    C. foolish
    D. unaware

9. MINIMIZE means the same as
   A. prolong
   B. reduce
   C. close
   D. continue

10. A DOCILE person is
    A. lazy
    B. bored
    C. assertive
    D. compliant

11. DISCREET means the same as
    A. heedless
    B. disrespectful
    C. unobtrusive
    D. brazen

12. PACK is to WOLVES as ORCHESTRA is to
    A. violin
    B. musicians
    C. symphony
    D. conductor

13. COMPOUND means the same as
    A. aggravate
    B. separate
    C. clarify
    D. improve

14. A CONTROVERSIAL issue is
    A. unquestionable

B. listless
C. disputed
D. uplifting

15. RELINQUISH means the same as
    A. grasp
    B. abdicate
    C. undertake
    D. challenge

## Spatial Ability
**Number of questions: 15**
**Time: 10 minutes**

*Directions: This section tests your ability to recognize the relationship between a form and its pattern. For each question, you will see a row of five pictures. If the first image on the left shows a PATTERN, you must choose which FORM (A, B, C, or D) could be created by folding the given pattern. If the first image on the left shows a FORM, you must choose which PATTERN (A, B, C, or D) would be needed to create that form.*

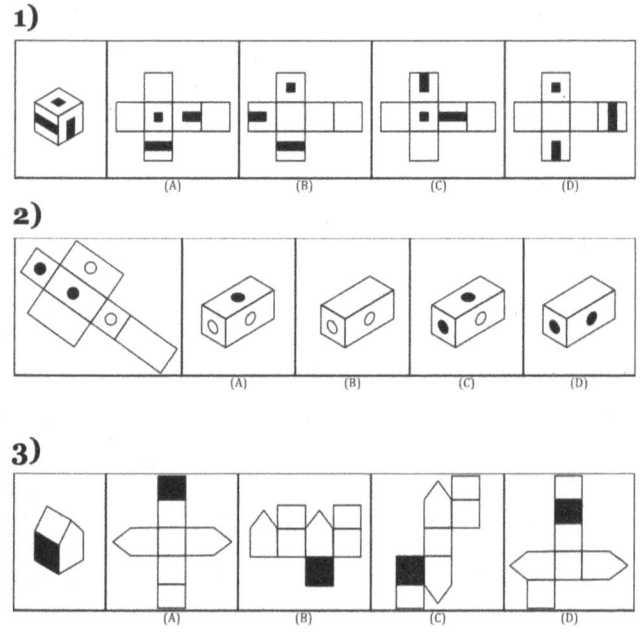

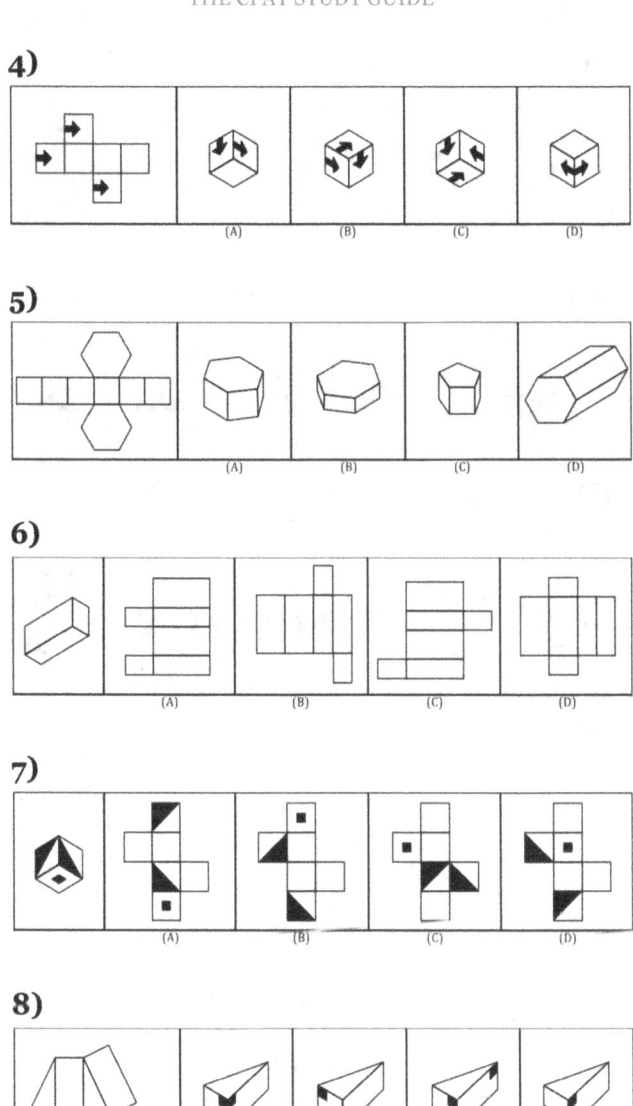

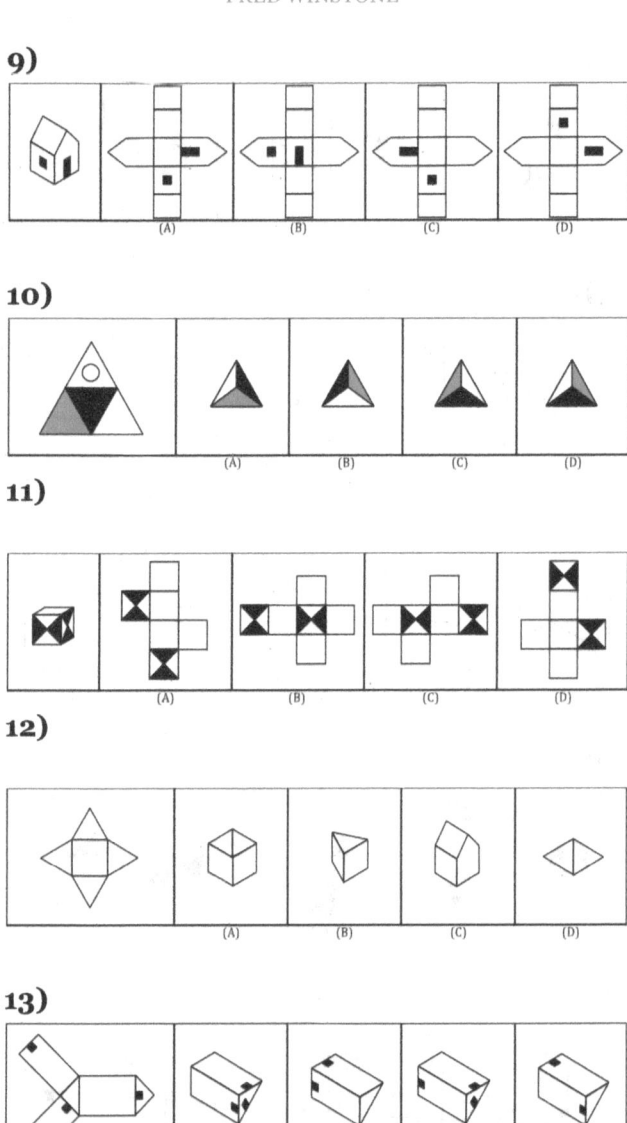

THE CFAT STUDY GUIDE

**14)**

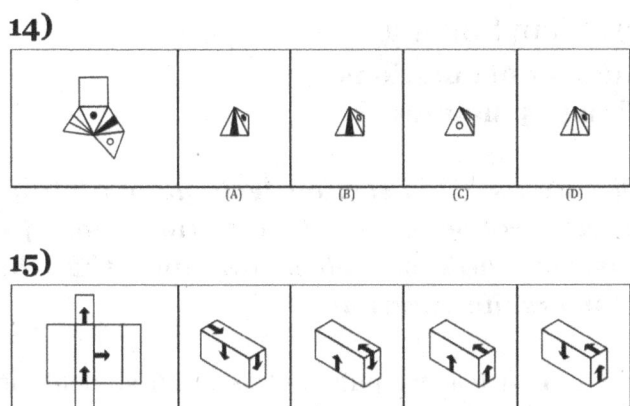

**15)**

# Problem Solving
**Number of questions: 30**
**Time: 45 minutes**

*Directions: This section tests your ability to solve problems. Each question has four answer choices. Select the one that best answers the question.*

1. A teacher puts a class of 29 students into groups of two or three students. What would be the smallest number of groups possible?
    E. 8
    F. 9
    G. 10
    H. 11

2. If $a = -3$, what is the value of $3a^2 + 2a - 4$?
    A. −91
    B. −37
    C. 17
    D. 71

3. How many hours are there in one leap year?
    A. 8,064
    B. 8,736
    C. 8,760
    D. 8,784

4. Where *a*, *b*, and *c*, are all positive numbers, *a* is twice as large as *b*, and *c* is equal to the product of *a* and *b*, then half of *c* is equal to
   A. $b$
   B. $b^2$
   C. $\frac{b}{2}$
   D. $-b$

5. A grocery store sells Red Delicious apples for $5.50 per kg and Honeycrisp apples for $8.60 per kg. If Dan buys 2.5 kg of apples, how much more would it cost to buy Honeycrisp apples than Red Delicious apples?
   A. $3.10
   B. $6.20
   C. $7.75
   D. $13.75

6. How many numbers less than 100 are multiples of both 5 and 3?
   A. 6
   B. 15
   C. 20
   D. 26

7. Which number comes next in the following sequence? 2, 10, 40, 120, 240...
   A. 240
   B. 360
   C. 400
   D. 480

8. A course allows a maximum of 40 students to enroll. If 32 of the spots are currently filled, what percentage of the spots are still available?
   A. 8%
   B. 20%
   C. 40%
   D. 80%

9. 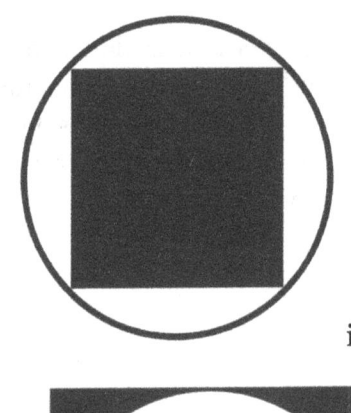 is to

as

# THE CFAT STUDY GUIDE

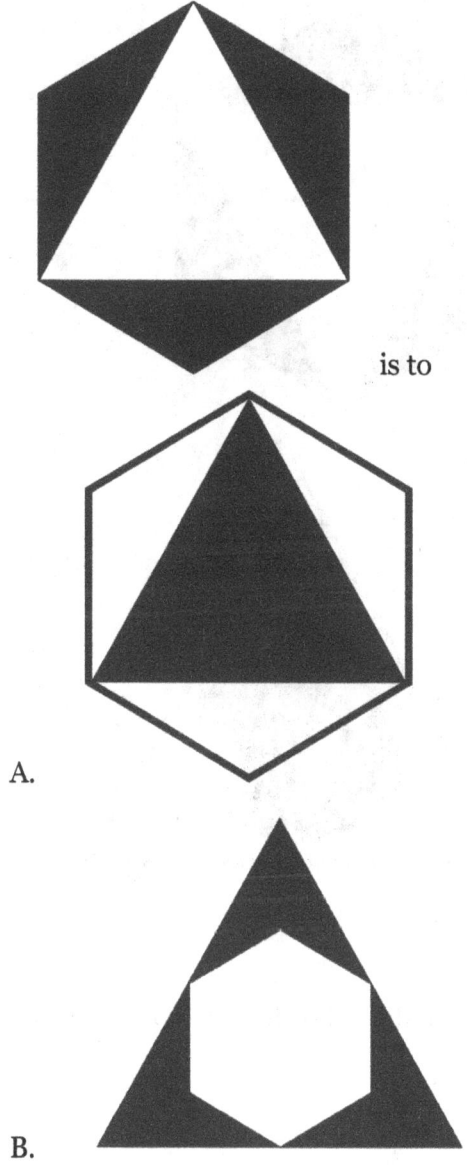

is to

A.

B.

C.

D.

10. Which of the following is NOT equal to the other three?
    A. $0.5^2$
    B. $\frac{1}{4}$
    C. 0.2
    D. 25%

11. What is the value of $(3 - 6)^2 + 2 \times 5 - 1$?
    A. 0
    B. 18
    C. 44
    D. 54

12. Evelyn purchased a sofa on sale for 30% off. If she paid $560, how much money did she save compared to the regular price?
    A. $168
    B. $240
    C. $392
    D. $800

13. Michelle can decorate three cupcakes in five minutes. At this rate, how many cupcakes can she decorate in one hour?
    A. 24
    B. 30
    C. 36
    D. 48

14. Four friends have dinner together at a restaurant. Their bill comes to $96. They decide on splitting the bill evenly and leaving a 20% tip. How much does each person pay?
    A. $19.20
    B. $24.20
    C. $28.80
    D. $29.00

15. What is the smallest positive four-digit integer that is divisible by 3?
    A. 1,000
    B. 1,002
    C. 1,012
    D. 1,200

16. Calculate the probability of rolling a number greater than 2 on a standard 6-sided dice?
    A. $\frac{1}{6}$
    B. $\frac{1}{3}$
    C. $\frac{1}{2}$
    D. $\frac{2}{3}$

17. Nick is installing square tiles that are 60 cm long on the floor of a rectangular room that measures 5.4 meters by 6 meters. How many tiles would he need to cover the entire floor?
    A. 80
    B. 90
    C. 110
    D. 120

18. Teresa leaves home at 7:20 and drives for 42 km at an average speed of 70 km per hour. What time does she arrive at her destination?
    A. 7:36
    B. 7:56
    C. 8:02
    D. 8:30

19. $\frac{2}{5}$ of the pens in Kaylee's bag are blue and the rest are black. What percentage of her pens are black?
    A. 20%
    B. 40%
    C. 60%
    D. 80%

20. If 25% of a number works out to 60, what is $\frac{1}{3}$ of the number?
    A. 5
    B. 20
    C. 65
    D. 80

21. A gymnastics class costs $80 per month per student. If more than one student from the same family enrolls, this monthly price is reduced by $5 per student. How much would it cost for two students from the same family to take the gymnastics class for six months?
    A. $450
    B. $750
    C. $900
    D. $950

22. The average of the numbers $a$ and $b$ is 23. The average of $a$, $b$, & $c$ is 27. What is the value of $c$?
    A. 4
    B. 35
    C. 42

D. 58

23. Jared needs the brake pads and rotors replaced for both rear wheels of his car. An automotive repair shop charges $110 per wheel for rotors, and brake pads are sold as a set for two wheels for $85. In addition, they charge $100 per hour for labour. If the repair takes 45 minutes for the shop to complete, what will Jared's total cost be?
    A. $295
    B. $380
    C. $405
    D. $465

24. Which of the following has the smallest value?
    A. 0.05
    B. $\frac{2}{50}$
    C. $0.3^2$
    D. $\frac{1}{10}$

25. The hardcover version of a book sells for $20, while the paperback version sells for $12. What is the percent savings for buying the paperback version instead of the hardcover?
    A. 8%
    B. 25%
    C. 40%
    D. 60%

26. Riley has a rock collection with a total of 36 rocks. The ratio of igneous to metamorphic to sedimentary rocks in her collection is 3:5:1. How many metamorphic rocks does she have?
    A. 5
    B. 7
    C. 12
    D. 20

27. There are three children in the Davis family. The youngest is half the age of the oldest. The middle child is 7 years old and is two years older than the youngest. What is the total of all of their ages (in years)?
    A. 17
    B. 18
    C. 22
    D. 30

28. One week in February, the high temperature in Toronto was 3°C for three days, 2°C one day, 1°C for two days, and 4°C one day. What was the average daily high temperature for the week (to the nearest tenth)?
    A. 1.7°C
    B. 2.1°C
    C. 2.4°C
    D. 3.2°C

29. Which number comes next in the following sequence? −24, 12, −6 ...
    A. −3

B. 3
C. 12
D. 18

30. A Canadian passport photo must measure 50 mm by 70 mm. What is the perimeter of the photo (in mm)?
    A. 120
    B. 240
    C. 1,200
    D. 3,500

# Chapter 10: Practice Test 1 Answers with Explanations
## Practice Test 1

### Verbal Skills

1. INQUIRE means the same as
    A. answer
    B. peddle
    C. ignore
    **D. investigate**

    The correct answer is (D), investigate. To *inquire* means to ask for information or to look into something. The best match is *investigate*. Choice (A) is incorrect because someone inquiring seeks, not provides, an answer. Choice (B) is incorrect because *peddle* means to sell, which is not the same as *inquire*. Choice (C) is incorrect because to *inquire* about something is not to *ignore* it but to give it attention through investigation.

2. BARTER means the same as
    **A. trade**
    B. return
    C. hoard
    D. bequeath

The correct answer is (A), trade. *Barter* means to exchange or trade goods. Choice (B) is incorrect because to *return* something would be to give it back, not trade it for something else. Choice (C) is incorrect because to *hoard* means to save or accumulate things, not trade them. Choice (D) is incorrect because to *bequeath* something is to give it away (usually in a will), not trade it.

3. FREEZING is to COOL as INFURIATING is to
    A. frigid
    **B. irksome**
    C. anger
    D. pleasant

The correct answer is (B), irksome. *Freezing* and *cool* are both words related to a cold temperature, but they differ in degree of intensity. *Freezing* describes a much more extreme cold than *cool*. Likewise, if something is *infuriating*, it is extremely bothersome, causing anger, whereas *irksome* refers to a more mild annoyance. Choice (A) is incorrect because while *frigid* connects to the cold-related words in the first part of the analogy, it does not fit with *infuriating*. Choice (C) is incorrect because *anger* is a noun, and an adjective is needed to complete the analogy. In addition, *anger* does not differ significantly enough in intensity from *infuriating*. Choice (D) is incorrect because *pleasant* would be the opposite of *infuriating* rather than a lesser degree of a similar adjective.

4. WITHER means the same as
   **A. shrivel**
   B. grow
   C. moisten
   D. brighten

The correct answer is (A), shrivel. To *wither* is to weaken or diminish, which is a good match for *shrivel*. Choice (B) is incorrect because something that withers gets smaller, not larger, so *grow* is an opposite. Choice (C) is incorrect because often, something that *withers* lacks moisture (dries up). Choice (D) is incorrect because *brighten* would indicate increased vitality, which is the opposite of *wither*.

5. LENIENT is the opposite of
   A. relaxed
   B. intelligent
   **C. strict**
   D. deceitful

The correct answer is (C), strict. *Lenient* means permissive or tolerant, which is the opposite of *strict*. Choice (A) is incorrect because *relaxed* can be a synonym for *lenient*, not the opposite. Choice (B) is incorrect because being *intelligent* does not indicate whether or not a person is lenient. Choice (D) is incorrect because to be *deceitful* is to intentionally mislead others, which is not the opposite of *lenient*.

6. SATISFIED means the same as
   **A. content**
   B. unhappy
   C. lazy
   D. ecstatic

The correct answer is (A), content. Someone who is *satisfied* is *content*–happy with what they have or their current situation. Choice (B) is incorrect because an *unhappy* person is dissatisfied. Choice (C) is incorrect because a person happy with what they have is not necessarily *lazy*. Choice (D) is incorrect because *ecstatic* means overwhelmingly joyful or excited, which is more extreme than *satisfied*.

7. IGUANA is to REPTILE as SHEEP is to
   A. goat
   **B. mammal**
   C. animal
   D. lizard

The correct answer is (B), mammal. Just as an *iguana* is a specific type of *reptile*, a *sheep* is a specific type of *mammal*. Choice (A) is incorrect because a *goat* is another type of mammal, not the category to which *sheep* belongs. Choice (C) is incorrect because *animal* is too broad. *Mammal* is the classification level equivalent to *reptile*. Choice (D) is incorrect because while an *iguana* is a type of *lizard*, this is unrelated to the *sheep*.

8. STATELY means the same as
    A. nonchalant
    B. small
    **C. dignified**
    D. aggressive

The correct answer is (C), dignified. Someone who is *stately* has a refined, noble, often impressive manner. *Dignified* is the best match. Choice (A) is incorrect because *nonchalant* means casual or carefree, which is not a good fit for *stately*. Choice (B) is incorrect because if *stately* is used to describe size, it refers to something large and grand, not *small*. Choice (D) is incorrect because to be *aggressive* would be inconsistent with the decorum expected of someone *stately*.

9. SIGHT is to EYESORE as SOUND is to
    **A. cacophony**
    B. melody
    C. instrument
    D. voice

The correct answer is (A), cacophony. An *eyesore* is an unpleasant *sight*, just as a *cacophony* is an unpleasant *sound*. Choice (B) is incorrect because *melody* generally has a positive connotation. Choices (C) and (D) are incorrect because *instrument* and *voice* refer to the source of a sound, not its quality.

10. PLACATE means the same as
    A. prepare
    B. entertain
    C. inspire
    **D. pacify**

The correct answer is (D), pacify. To *placate* means to soothe someone or appease them to calm them down. *Pacify* is the best match. Choice (A) is incorrect because *placate* is unrelated to preparation. Choice (B) is incorrect because while providing entertainment could be an example of a way to pacify someone, it is not a direct synonym for the word. Choice (C) is incorrect because *placate* is unrelated to inspiration.

11. To SUBSTANTIATE a claim means to
    A. disprove
    **B. confirm**
    C. undermine
    D. argue
    E.

The correct answer is (B), confirm. To *substantiate* a claim is to provide evidence to support it, helping confirm its validity. Choice (A) is incorrect because substantiation helps prove, not *disprove*, a claim. Choice (C) is incorrect because to *undermine* a claim would be to make it seem less trustworthy, which is the opposite of what it means to substantiate a claim. Choice (D) is incorrect because you can *argue* for or against a claim, so this is not specific enough to be a good match for *substantiate*.

12. DECREE means the same as
    A. suggestion
    B. increment
    C. question
    **D. proclamation**

The correct answer is (D), proclamation. A *decree* is an official announcement or mandate. The best match is *proclamation*. Choice (A) is incorrect because a *decree* is an order, not a *suggestion*. Choice (B) is incorrect because a decree is unrelated to an *increment*, or additional amount. If you picked (B), you might have mistaken *decree* for *degree*, which looks similar but has a very different meaning. Choice (C) is incorrect because a decree is a statement, not a question.

13. TRICKLE is to DELUGE as BREEZE is to
    A. flood
    B. gale
    **C. tornado**

D. rain

The correct answer is (C), tornado. The relationship between *trickle* and *deluge* is one of intensity. A trickle refers to a small flow of water, while a deluge is a flood. Likewise, a *breeze* is a very light wind, while a *tornado* is an extremely strong wind. Choice (A) is incorrect because while *flood* is a synonym for *deluge*, it does not relate to *breeze* in a similar way as *trickle* does to *deluge*. Choice (B) is incorrect because *gale* is a synonym for *breeze*, not a wind of much greater intensity. Choice (D) is incorrect because *rain* is more closely related to *trickle* and *deluge* than to *breeze*.

14. PERCEIVE means the same as
    A. obtain
    B. avoid
    **C. notice**
    D. create

The correct answer is (C), notice. To *perceive* is to see or observe something. *Notice* is the best match. Choice (A) is incorrect because to *obtain* means to get something, which is not a good match for *perceive*. Choice (B) is incorrect because *avoid* means to stay away from something, which is not a good match for *perceive*. Choice (D) is incorrect because *create* means to make something new rather than to observe something that already exists.

15. Someone who DITHERS is
    A. hasty
    **B. indecisive**
    C. confident
    D. enthusiastic

The correct answer is (B), indecisive. If someone *dithers*, they hesitate because they can't make up their mind. *Indecisive* (unable to decide) is a good fit. Choice (A) is incorrect because *hasty* means to act quickly and without much thought, which is the opposite of dithering. Choice (C) is incorrect because someone who *dithers* lacks confidence. Choice (D) is incorrect because dithering typically makes someone fretful, not *enthusiastic*.

# Spatial Ability

**1)**

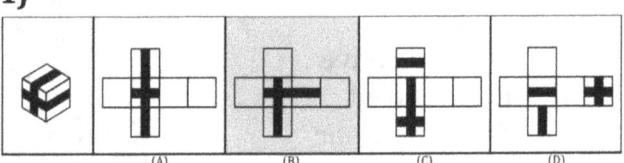

**2)**

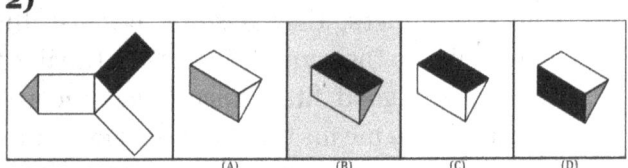

**3)**

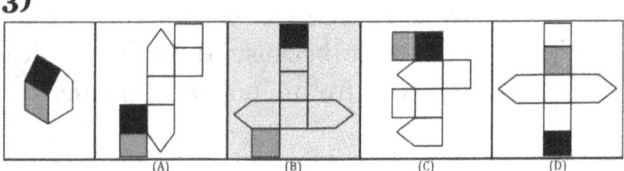

**4)**

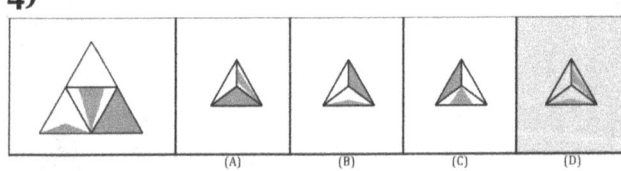

**5)**

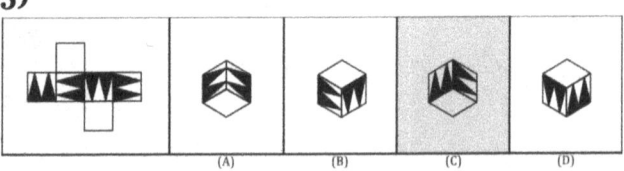

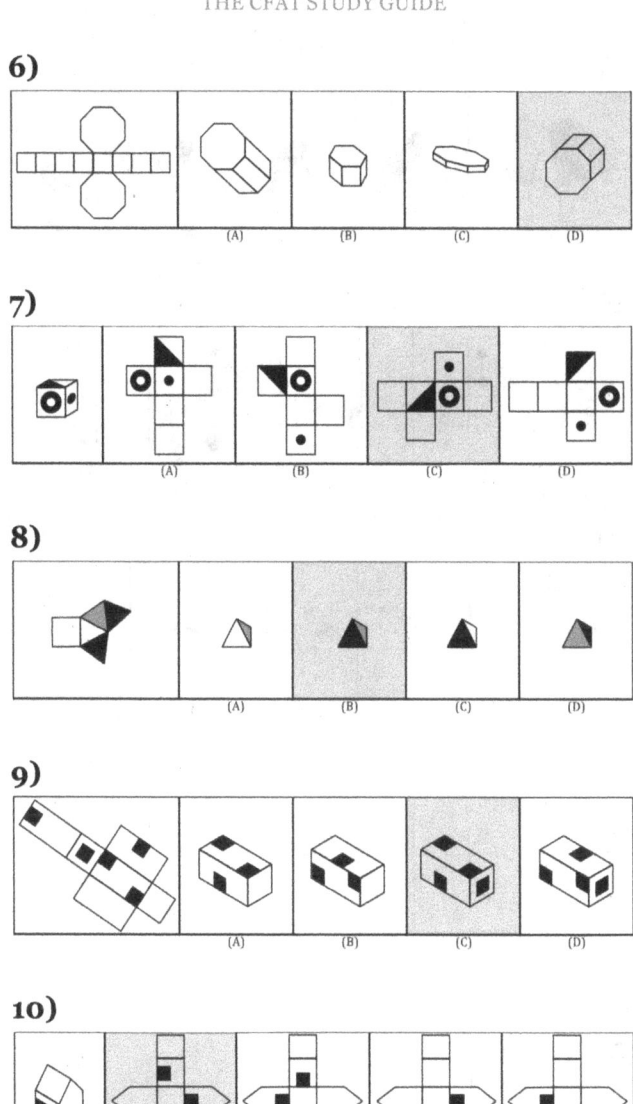

**11)**

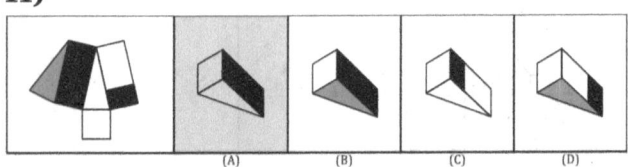

**12)**

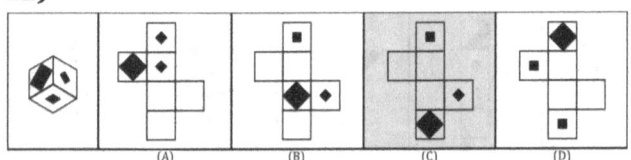

**13)**

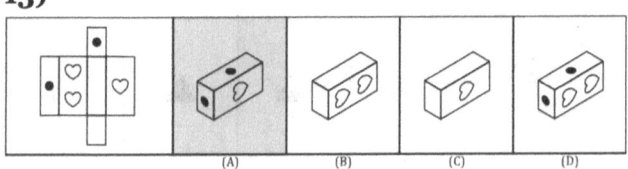

**14)**

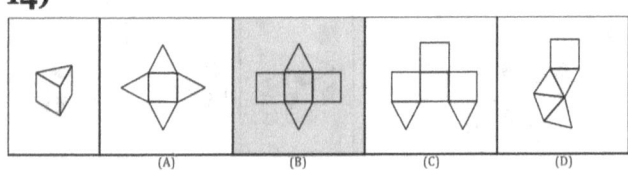

**15)**

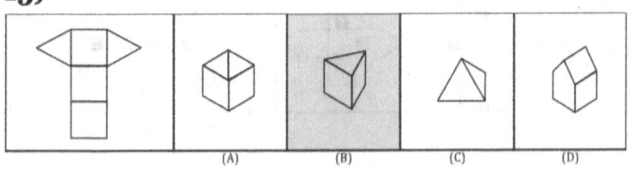

## Problem Solving

1. If a car travels on a road at an average speed of 84 kilometres per hour, how far will the car travel in 25 minutes?
   - A. 4 km
   - B. 18 km
   - C. 26 km
   - **D. 35 km**

   The correct answer is (D), 35 km. The car's speed is 84 km/h, so it travels 84 km every 60 minutes. Set up a proportion to solve, letting $x$ represent the distance travelled.
   $$\frac{84\ km}{60\ min} = \frac{x}{25\ min}$$
   $$60x = 84(25)$$
   $$60x = 2100$$
   $$x = 35$$
   The car travels 35 km in 25 minutes.

2. Daniel and Maya both arrived at work at exactly 8:00 yesterday. Daniel left his house at 7:42, but it took Daniel twice as long to get to work as it took Maya. Assuming it takes her the same amount of time to get to work each day, what time will Maya arrive at work tomorrow if she leaves her house at 7:49?
   - A. 7:51
   - **B. 7:58**
   - C. 8:00
   - D. 8:07

The correct answer is (B), 7:58. It took Daniel 18 minutes to get to work. This is twice as long as it took Maya, so she took 18 ÷ 2 = 9 minutes to get to work. Tomorrow, if she leaves at 7:49, she will arrive 9 minutes later, at 7:58.

3. A certain type of army battalion consists of five companies, each of which contains three platoons. How many platoons are in two such battalions?
    A. 10
    B. 15
    C. 16
    **D. 30**

The correct answer is (D), 30. Each battalion has 5 × 3 = 15 platoons, so two battalions would have 15 × 2 = 30 platoons.

4.  is to

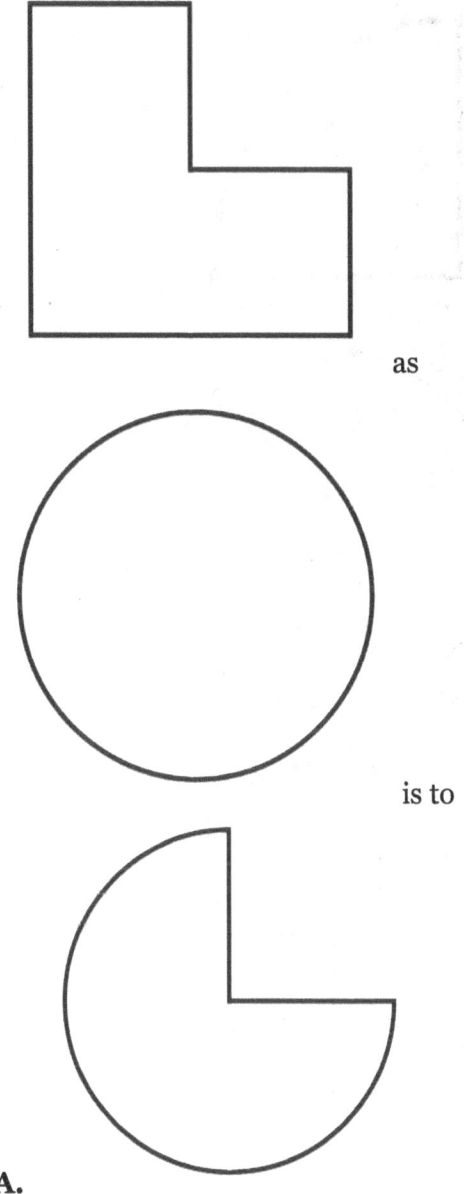

as

is to

**A.**

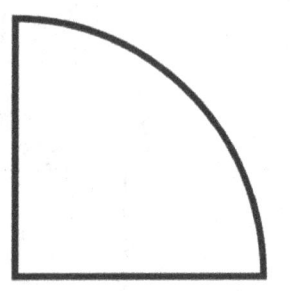

B.

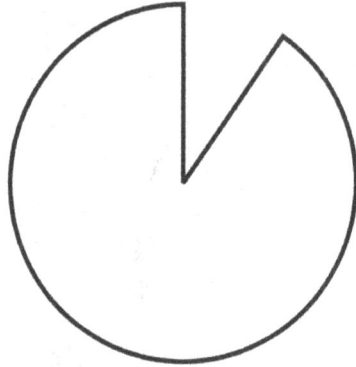

C.

D.

The correct answer is (A). The first pair of shapes consists of a square and a square missing its top-right quarter. Similarly, choice (A) shows a circle with the top-right quarter missing.

5. 64% of the students currently enrolled in a class are female, and the rest are male. If one male student were to drop out of the class, the males would make up exactly one-third of the class. How many students are currently in the class?
   A. 16
   B. 24
   **C. 25**
   D. 36

The correct answer is (C), 25. If 64% of the current students are female, then 100% − 64% = 36% of the students are male. As a fraction, this is equal to $\frac{36}{100}$, which reduces to $\frac{9}{25}$. Let $m$ be the number of male students currently enrolled in the class, and let $s$ be the total number of students currently enrolled. We can set up the following equation to represent the students currently enrolled in the class: $m = \frac{9}{25}s$. If one male student dropped out, the number of male students would be $m - 1$ and the total number of students would be $s - 1$. We also know that the males would make up $\frac{1}{3}$ of the students, so we can create the equation

$m - 1 = \frac{1}{3}(s - 1)$. Distributing gives $m - 1 = \frac{1}{3}s - \frac{1}{3}$. Adding 1 to both sides gives $m = \frac{1}{3}s + \frac{2}{3}$. Now we have two equations both solved for $m$, so we can set them equal to each other to solve for $s$.

$$\frac{9}{25}s = \frac{1}{3}s + \frac{2}{3}$$
$$\frac{9}{25}s - \frac{1}{3}s = \frac{2}{3}$$
$$\frac{27}{75}s - \frac{25}{75}s = \frac{2}{3}$$
$$\frac{2}{75}s = \frac{2}{3}$$
$$s = \frac{2}{3} \times \frac{75}{2}$$
$$s = 25$$

There are currently 25 students enrolled in the class.

6. Which number comes next in the following sequence? 2, 6, 18, 54, ...
    A. 58
    B. 90
    C. 108
    **D. 162**

The correct answer is (D), 162. Each term is worked out by multiplying the previous term by 3, so the next term would be $54 \times 3 = 162$.

7. Three friends share a pizza and, between them, eat the entire pizza. Ben eats 50% more

pizza than Alex, and Carlos eats the same amount of pizza as Ben. What portion of the pizza does Alex eat?

A. $\frac{1}{5}$

**B.** $\frac{1}{4}$

C. $\frac{1}{3}$

D. $\frac{1}{2}$

The correct answer is (B), $\frac{1}{4}$. Let $a$ represent the portion of the pizza Alex eats. If Ben eats 50% more pizza than Alex, then he eats 150% of Alex's portion, so we can represent Ben's portion with $1.5a$. Carlos eats the same amount as Ben, so his portion can also be represented by $1.5a$. We can create an equation where these three portions add up to 1, representing the whole pizza: $a + 1.5a + 1.5a = 1$. Combining like terms gives $4a = 1$, and dividing both sides by 4 gives $a = \frac{1}{4}$. So, Alex ate $\frac{1}{4}$ of the pizza.

8. What is $\frac{1}{5}$ divided by 0.3?

A. $\frac{3}{50}$

B. $\frac{1}{15}$

C. $\frac{3}{5}$

**D.** $\frac{2}{3}$

The correct answer is (D), $\frac{2}{3}$. Since the answer choices are fractions, start by converting the decimal to a fraction: $0.3 = \frac{3}{10}$. Now divide, remembering that dividing by a fraction is the same task as multiplying by its reciprocal. $\frac{1}{5} \div \frac{3}{10} = \frac{1}{5} \times \frac{10}{3} = \frac{10}{15}$, which reduces to $\frac{2}{3}$.

9. Which of the following would be the next two shapes in the pattern below?

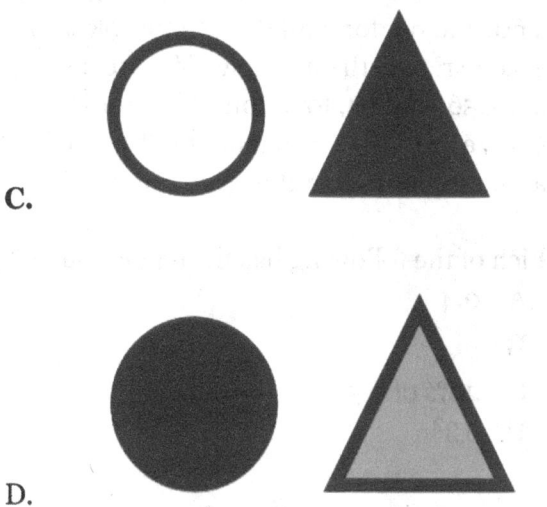

**C.**

**D.**

The correct answer is (C). The colours repeat the pattern black, grey, white, black, and so on, while the shapes alternate between triangles and circles. Since the last shape in the given pattern is a grey triangle, the next two colours must be white and black, in that order, and the shapes must be a circle followed by a triangle.

10. How many more multiples of 4 than multiples of 8 are there between 21 and 67?
    **A. 5**
    B. 6
    C. 11
    D. 17

The correct answer is (A), 5. The multiples of 4 in that range are 24, 28, 32, 36, 40, 44, 48, 52, 56, 60, and 64, for a total of 11 multiples. In the same range, the multiples of 8 are 24, 32, 40, 48, 56, and 64, for a total of 6 multiples. So, there are 11 − 6 = 5 more multiples of 4 than multiples of 8 in the given range.

11. Which of the following has the highest value?
    A. 0.4
    **B.** $\frac{3}{5}$
    C. 20% of 0.5
    D. $0.3^2$

The correct answer is (B), $\frac{3}{5}$. Convert each answer choice to a decimal to make them easier to compare. Choice (A) is already a decimal, 0.4. Choice (B), $\frac{3}{5}$, is equal to $\frac{6}{10}$, so expressed as a decimal, it is 0.6. For choice (C), determine what 20% of 0.5 is by multiplying by 0.2. This gives 0.5 × 0.2 = 0.1. For choice (D), $0.3^2$ = 0.3 × 0.3 = 0.09. Comparing these four answer choices–0.4, 0.6, 0.2, and 0.1–the largest is 0.6, choice (B).

12. Marcy works out five times each week. How many times does she work out each year?
    A. 60
    B. 190
    **C. 260**
    D. 365

The correct answer is (C), 260. There are 52 weeks in each year, so Marcy works out $52 \times 5 = 260$ times per year.

13. Luke worked 34 hours over the course of five days last week. On average, how many hours did he work each of those days?
    A. 6 hours and 8 minutes
    B. 6 hours and 25 minutes
    C. 6 hours and 34 minutes
    **D. 6 hours and 48 minutes**

The correct answer is (D), 6 hours and 48 minutes. Divide 34 hours by five days to find the hours per day: $34 \div 5 = 6.8$. So, Luke worked 6 hours plus 0.8 hours, or $\frac{8}{10}$ of an hour. Since there are 60 minutes in each hour, you can multiply both the top and bottom of that fraction by 6 to find the equivalent fraction over 60. $\frac{8}{10} \times \frac{6}{6} = \frac{48}{60}$. So, 0.8 hours is equal to 48 minutes. Luke worked an average of 6 hours and 48 minutes per day.

14. Jamal wants to buy a cell phone that normally costs $500. The phone is currently on sale for 15% off. What is the sale price of the phone?
    A. $75
    B. $375
    **C. $425**
    D. $485

The correct answer is ⓒ, $425. 15% of $500 is $500 × 0.15 = $75, so the sale price of the phone is $500 − $75 = $425.

15. Anna has a candlemaking business. She buys $300 worth of supplies. If each candle sells for $12, what is the minimum number of candles she must sell in order to make a profit?
    A. 24
    B. 25
    **C. 26**
    D. 27

The correct answer is (C), 26. To recover precisely the $300 cost, Anna must sell $300 ÷ $12 = 25 candles. To make a profit, she must sell at least one more candle than that, for a total of 26.

16. In a survey of 50 households, 60% of the households owned a dog, a cat, or both. If 19 of the households surveyed owned a dog and 23 owned a cat, how many households owned both a dog and a cat?
    A. 8
    **B. 12**
    C. 15
    D. 19

The correct answer is (B), 12. If 60% of the 50 households owned a dog, cat, or both, that means 50 × 0.6 = 30 households owned a dog, a cat, or both. If 19 owned a dog and 23 owned a cat, that makes a total of 42, which is more than the number of households with dogs or cats. So, some of these households must own both a cat and a dog. 42 − 30 = 12 households own both a dog and a cat.

17. What is the missing number in the following sequence?

$$-1, 2, -4, ?, -16, 32$$

   A. −8
   B. −7
   **C. 8**
   D. 12

The correct answer is (C), 8. Each term results from multiplying the previous term by −2, so the term that follows 4 would be (−4)(−2) = 8.

18. If 20% of a number is 45, what is the number?

   A. 9
   B. 65
   **C. 225**
   D. 900

The correct answer is (C), 225. You can set up a proportion using the percent formula to solve.

$$\frac{\%}{100} = \frac{part}{whole}$$

$$\frac{20}{100} = \frac{45}{x}$$
$$20x = 100(45)$$
$$20x = 4500$$
$$x = 225$$

19. A bag happens to contain 3 red marbles, 4 blue marbles, and 5 green marbles. What is the probability that a marble pulled from the bag will NOT be red?

    A. $\frac{1}{9}$

    B. $\frac{1}{4}$

    C. $\frac{1}{3}$

    **D. $\frac{3}{4}$**

The correct answer is (D), $\frac{3}{4}$. There are $4 + 5 = 9$ marbles that are not red out of a total of $3 + 4 + 5 = 12$ marbles. So, the probability of pulling a marble that is not red is $\frac{9}{12}$, which reduces to $\frac{3}{4}$.

20. Michelle is 16 years old. Jordan's age is four years less than twice Michelle's age. How old will Jordan be two years from now?

    A. 26

    B. 28

    **C. 30**

D. 32

The correct answer is (C), 30. Right now, Michelle is 16, and Jordan is four years less than twice that, so Jordan is 16(2) − 4 = 32 − 4 = 28 years old. Two years from now, Jordan will be 28 + 2 = 30 years old.

21. Brand A sells a box of eight granola bars for $2.72. Brand B sells a box of six granola bars for $2.28. Brand C sells a box of 16 granola bars for $5.12. Brand D sells a box of 12 granola bars for $3.36. Which brand has the lowest price per granola bar?
    A. Brand A
    B. Brand B
    C. Brand C
    **D. Brand D**

The correct answer is (D), Brand D. Divide the price by the number of granola bars to find each brand's price per granola bar. Brand A's price is $2.72 ÷ 8 = $0.34 per granola bar. Brand B's price is $2.28 ÷ 6 = $0.38 per granola bar. Brand C's price is $5.12 ÷ 16 = $0.32 per granola bar. Brand D's price is $3.36 ÷ 12 = $0.28 per granola bar, making Brand D's price per bar the lowest.

22. $\left(\frac{1}{5} \div \frac{3}{4}\right) - \left(\frac{3}{5} \div 6\right) = ?$

   A. $\frac{1}{15}$
   
   **B.** $\frac{1}{6}$
   
   C. $\frac{7}{30}$
   
   D. $\frac{19}{60}$

The correct answer is (B), $\frac{1}{6}$. Remember, dividing by a fraction is the same task as multiplying by its reciprocal (which is 1 divided by itself)..

$$\left(\frac{1}{5} \div \frac{3}{4}\right) - \left(\frac{3}{5} \div 6\right) =$$
$$\left(\frac{1}{5} \times \frac{4}{3}\right) - \left(\frac{3}{5} \times \frac{1}{6}\right) =$$
$$\frac{4}{15} - \frac{3}{30}$$

From there, find a common denominator (30) to perform the subtraction, then reduce it to its lowest terms.

$$\frac{8}{30} - \frac{3}{30} = \frac{5}{30} = \frac{1}{6}$$

23. It takes the planet Mercury 59 days to complete one rotation on its axis, and it takes 88 days for Mercury to complete one orbit around the Sun. In the time it takes Mercury

to orbit the Sun three times, how many times will Mercury make a complete rotation on its axis?

**A. 4**
B. 9
C. 27
D. 87

The correct answer is (A), 4. Mercury will orbit the Sun three times in 88 × 3 = 264 days. In that time, Mercury will rotate approximately 264 ÷ 59 = 4.47 times, so the number of complete rotations is 4.

24. $2^2 + (13 - 5) \times 3 = ?$

    A. 2
    B. 15
    **C. 28**
    D. 36

The correct answer is (C), 28. Remember to solve using the order of operations: BEMDAS (Brackets, Exponent, Multiplication/Division, Addition/Subtraction).

$$2^2 + (13 - 5) \times 3 =$$
$$2^2 + 8 \times 3 =$$
$$4 + 8 \times 3 =$$
$$4 + 24 = 28$$

25. The area of a circle is expressed by the formula $A = 3.14r^2$, where $A$ is the area and $r$ is the radius. What is the radius of a circle whose area is 28.26 cm²?
    A. 2 cm
    **B. 3 cm**
    C. 4.5 cm
    D. 5.5 cm

The correct answer is (B), 3 cm. Plug the given area into the formula and solve for the radius.
$$A = 3.14r^2$$
$$28.26 = 3.14r^2$$
$$9 = r^2$$
$$3 = r$$
The radius of the circle is 3 cm.


26. Joyce takes out a $5,000 loan with a simple interest rate of 4% per year. If she pays back the loan in 3 years, how much will she have paid in total?
    A. $600
    B. $5,200
    **C. $5,600**
    D. $5,800

The correct answer is (C), $5,600. First, find the total interest paid by multiplying the principal amount ($5,000) by the interest rate (4%, or 0.04) and the time (3 years): $I =$ $5,000 \times 0.04 \times 3 = \$600$. Then, add the amount of interest paid to the original amount of the loan to find the total: $5,000 + $600 = $5,600.

27. On a map, the cities of Toronto and Ottawa are 11.7 cm apart. In real life, the cities are approximately 351 km apart. If the real-life distance between Toronto and Kingston is approximately 243 km, how far apart will they be on the map?
    A. 7.5 cm
    **B. 8.1 cm**
    C. 9.4 cm
    D. 10.3 cm

The correct answer is (B), 8.1 cm. Set up a proportion to solve.
$$\frac{351\ km}{11.7\ cm} = \frac{243\ km}{x\ cm}$$
$$351x = 243 \times 11.7$$
$$351x = 2843.1$$
$$x = 8.1$$
The distance between Toronto and Kingston on the map will be 8.1 cm.

28. Calculate the surface area of a box that is 15 cm long, 10 cm wide, and 6 cm high?
    A. 300 cm²
    B. 500 cm²
    **C. 600 cm²**

D. 900 cm²

The correct answer is (C), 600 cm². A box is a rectangular prism, and the surface area is simply the sum of the areas of the prism's six sides. These sides are in 3 identical pairs, so the surface area can be expressed as $SA = 2lw + 2wh + 2lh$. Plug in the given values to solve.

$$SA = 2lw + 2wh + 2lh$$
$$SA = 2(15 \times 10) + 2(10 \times 6) + 2(15 \times 6)$$
$$SA = 2(150) + 2(60) + 2(90)$$
$$SA = 300 + 120 + 180$$
$$SA = 600$$

The surface area is 600 cm².

29. If 15% of a number is 27, what is $\frac{2}{3}$ of the same number?
    A. 90
    **B. 120**
    C. 180
    D. 270

The correct answer is (B), 120. You can set up a proportion using the percent formula to solve for the number.

$$\frac{\%}{100} = \frac{part}{whole}$$
$$\frac{15}{100} = \frac{27}{x}$$
$$15x = 2700$$

$$x = 180$$

From there, the question asks for $\frac{2}{3}$ of that number, so $180 \times \frac{2}{3} = 120$.

30. Kathy can type 75 words per minute. If she begins typing at 9:25 and doesn't stop, at what time will she type her 1,000th word?
    - A. 9:37
    - **B. 9:38**
    - C. 9:39
    - D. 9:40

The correct answer is (B), 9:38. Dividing 1,000 words by the rate of 75 words per minute, it will take Kathy 13.3 minutes to type 1,000 words. Kathy will type the 1,000th word before the 14-minute mark, so she will finish 13 minutes after she starts, which is 9:38.

# Chapter 11: Practice Test 2 Answers With Explanations

## Verbal Skills

1. OUTCOME means the same as
   A. origin
   B. exit
   C. purpose
   **D. result**

   The correct answer is (D), result. An *outcome* is an effect or consequence. The best match is *result*. Choice (A) is incorrect because *origin* refers to a cause rather than an effect. Choice (B) is incorrect because an *exit*, or way out, is not related to *outcome*. Choice (C) is incorrect because *purpose*, or reason, is more closely associated with a cause than an effect.

2. FORTUNATE is to LUCK as HAPLESS is to
   A. happiness
   **B. calamity**
   C. stability
   D. triumph

The correct answer is (B), calamity. Someone who is *fortunate*, or lucky, experiences luck. Likewise, someone *hapless*, or unlucky, experiences *calamity*, or misfortune. Choice (A) is incorrect because being *hapless* (unlucky) does not bring happiness. Choice (C) is incorrect because someone unlucky does not necessarily experience *stability*. Choice (D) is incorrect because being *hapless* brings negative results, not a *triumph* or victory.

3. SKEPTICISM means the same as
   **A. doubt**
   B. decisiveness
   C. bitterness
   D. certainty

The correct answer is (A), doubt. *Skepticism* is being unsure or mistrustful. *Doubt* is a good match. Choice (B) is incorrect because a skeptical person is not very decisive. Choice (C) is incorrect because a skeptical person is not necessarily bitter, or resentful. Choice (D) is incorrect because *certainty* is the opposite of *skepticism*.

4. DEVISE means the same as
   A. destroy
   B. trick
   C. separate
   **D. formulate**

The correct answer is (D), formulate. *Devise* means to come up with something, such as a plan. *Formulate* is a good match. Choice (A) is incorrect because *devise* involves creating something, not destroying it. Choice (B) is incorrect because *devise* does not necessarily indicate a deceptive intent. Choice (C) is incorrect because *devise* does not relate to separation.

5. WORDS are to AUTHOR as NOTES are to
    A. performer
    B. article
    **C. composer**
    D. symphony

The correct answer is (C), composer. An *author* creates their works using *words*. Similarly, a *composer* creates music using *notes*. Choice (A) is incorrect because a *performer* may play notes, but a composer writes them as an author writes words. Choice (B) is incorrect because *article* may relate to *words* and *author* but not to notes. Choice (D) is incorrect because while *notes* may be part of a *symphony*, this analogy requires a person to complete it.

6. MOTIF means the same as
    A. reason
    B. disorder
    C. distraction
    **D. pattern**

The correct answer is (D), pattern. A *motif* is a recurring theme or *pattern*. Choice (A) is incorrect because a *reason* is a cause or motivation, not a theme. Choice (B) is incorrect because a *motif* brings order, not disorder. Choice (C) is incorrect because a *motif* is a central theme or pattern, not a *distraction*.

7. ATROCIOUS is the opposite of
    A. outrageous
    **B. wonderful**
    C. terrible
    D. mundane

The correct answer is (B), wonderful. *Atrocious* means very bad, so its opposite is very good– *wonderful*. Choices (A) and (C) are incorrect because *outrageous* and *terrible* can be synonyms for *atrocious*, not opposites. Choice (D) is incorrect because *mundane* means boring, which is more of a neutral term than the positive term needed for the opposite of *atrocious*.

8. CRUCIAL means the same as
    **A. necessary**
    B. worthless
    C. detracting
    D. available

The correct answer is (A), necessary. Something *crucial* is needed and important.

*Necessary* is a good fit. Choice (B) is incorrect because *worthless*, or unimportant, means the opposite of *crucial*. Choice (C) is incorrect because *detracting* means criticizing, which is not a synonym for *crucial*. Choice (D) is incorrect because while you might hope that something *crucial* will be *available* when you need it, this is different from what the word itself means. *Crucial* refers to something's importance, not whether or not it is accessible.

9. TENACIOUS means the same as
    A. fearful
    **B. determined**
    C. unreliable
    D. friendly

The correct answer is (B), determined. A *tenacious* person is strong and persistent. *Determined* is a good match. Choice (A) is incorrect because *tenacious* people tend to show little fear. Choice (C) is incorrect because a *tenacious* person is steadfast, not *unreliable*. Choice (D) is incorrect because *tenacious* does not indicate whether or not a person is friendly.

10. A DISTRAUGHT person is
    A. calm
    B. ambitious
    C. apathetic
    **D. upset**

The correct answer is (D), upset. *Distraught* means distressed or very *upset*. Choice (A) is incorrect because *calm* is the opposite of *distraught*. Choice (B) is incorrect because someone *ambitious* desires success, which is not related to being *distraught*. Choice (C) is incorrect because someone *apathetic* does not care, while someone *distraught* cares greatly.

11. HAPHAZARD means the same as
    A. perilous
    B. systematic
    **C. random**
    D. unsuccessful

The correct answer is (C), random. *Haphazard* means disorderly or done without a plan. *Random* is a good fit. Choice (A) is incorrect because *haphazard* does not necessarily refer to something *perilous*, or dangerous. Choice (B) is incorrect because *systematic*, or highly organized, is the opposite of *haphazard*. Choice (D) is incorrect because something done haphazardly may or may not be successful.

12. CAR is to STEERING WHEEL as HORSE is to
    A. rider
    **B. reins**
    C. animal
    D. saddle

The correct answer is (B), reins. A *steering wheel* is what the driver uses to direct a car's motion. Likewise, a rider uses *reins* to direct a horse. Choice (A) is incorrect because a horse's *rider* would be analogous to a car's driver, not the steering wheel. Choice (C) is incorrect because a *horse* is a type of *animal*, and a *steering wheel* is not a type of *car*. Choice (D) is incorrect because while a saddle is a tool used when riding a horse, it does not direct the horse as the steering wheel does to the car.

13. SCARCE means the same as
    **A. rare**
    B. afraid
    C. frequent
    D. useless

The correct answer is (A), rare. If something is *scarce*, there is not enough of it to meet a need. It is *rare*. Choice (B) is incorrect because *scarce* refers to something's availability, not whether it is fearful. Choice (C) is incorrect because *frequent* is the opposite of *scarce*. Choice (D) is incorrect because *scarce* typically refers to something needed and useful but hard to find.

14. A TEDIOUS task is
    A. entertaining
    B. demanding
    **C. dull**

D. unpredictable

The correct answer is (C), dull. A task described as *tedious* is boring and often monotonous. *Dull* is a good match. Choice (A) is incorrect because a *tedious* task is boring, not *entertaining* or fun. Choice (B) is incorrect because *tedious* tasks are not typically difficult to perform; rather, they are tiresome because they are boring and repetitive. Choice (D) is incorrect because *tedious* indicates repetitiveness, not unpredictability.

15. ARID means the same as
    A. spirited
    **B. dry**
    C. proud
    D. abundant

The correct answer is (B), dry. *Arid*, a term often used to describe deserts, means *dry* or barren. Choice (A) is incorrect because if *arid* were used to describe a person, it would indicate that they are lifeless, which is the opposite of *spirited*. Choice (C) is incorrect because pride is unrelated to dryness. Choice (D) is incorrect because *abundant* means plentiful, whereas an *arid* place is typically relatively empty.

# Spatial Ability Practice 2
**1)**

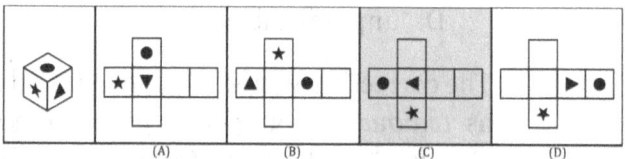

**2)**

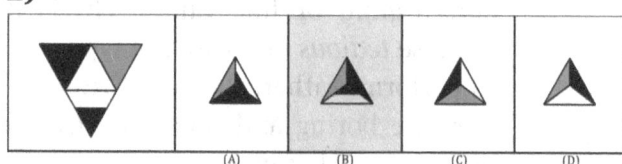

**3)**

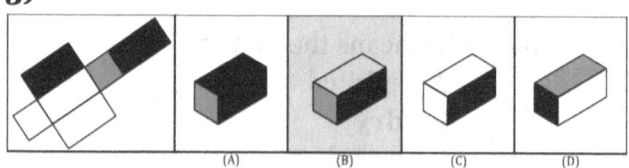

**4)**

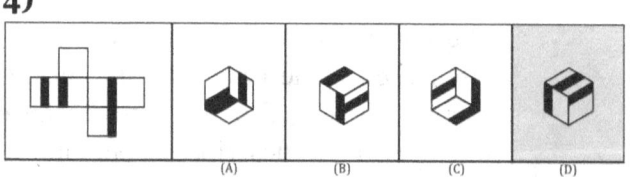

**5)**

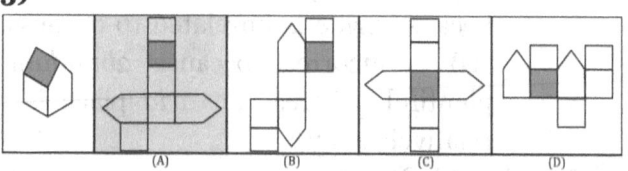

**6)**

# THE CFAT STUDY GUIDE

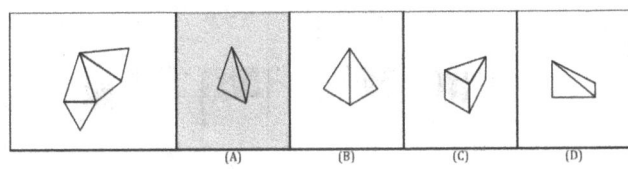

**7)**

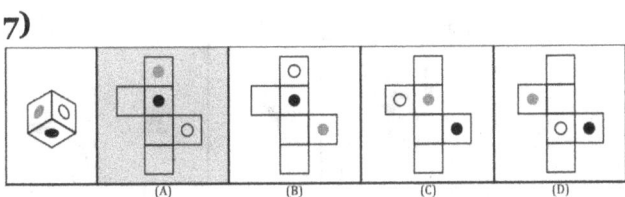

**8)**

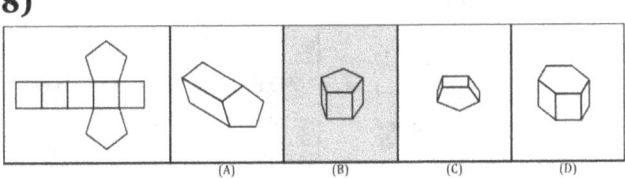

**9)**

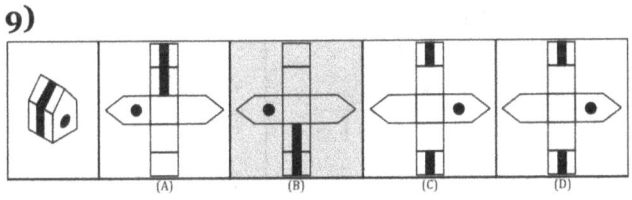

**10)**

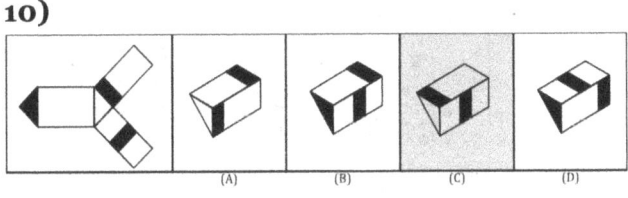

**11)**

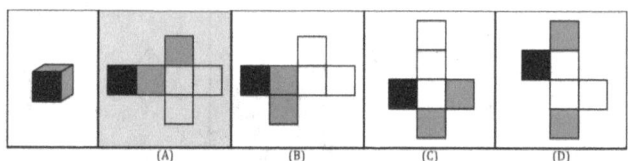

**12)**

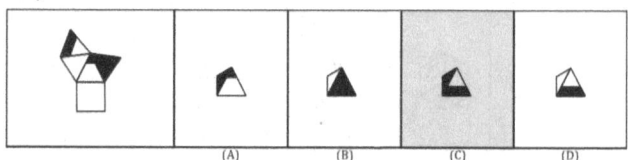

**13)**

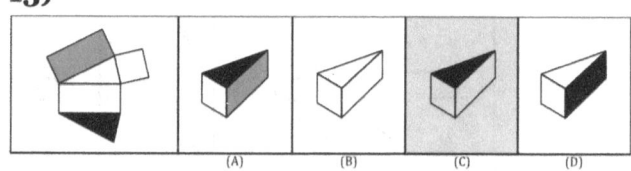

**14)**

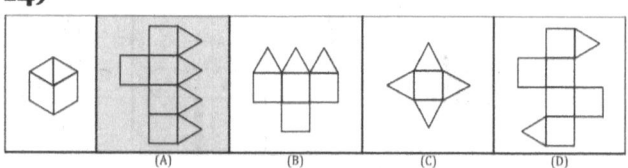

**15)**

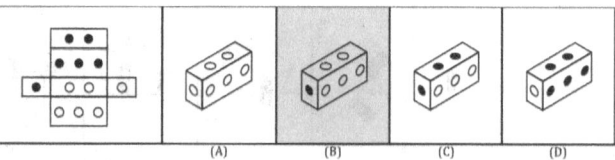

# Problem Solving

1. Rachel drove 45 km, and her vehicle's gasoline consumption averaged 8 L/100 km. If gasoline costs $1.20 per litre, how much did the gasoline for this trip cost?
    A. $3.00
    B. $3.60
    **C. $4.32**
    D. $6.75

The correct answer is (C), $4.32. First, set up a proportion to find the litres of gasoline used on the trip.
$$\frac{8\,L}{100\,km} = \frac{x}{45\,km}$$
$$100x = 8 \times 45$$
$$100x = 360$$
$$x = 3.6$$
From there, multiply by $1.20 per litre to find the total cost of the gasoline: $3.6 \times \$1.20 = \$4.32$.

2. The student-to-teacher ratio at a school is 18:1. Which of these could be the total number of students and teachers at the school?
    A. 324
    B. 378
    **C. 418**
    D. 450

The correct answer is (C), 418. Since there are 18 students for every one teacher at the school, the total number of students and teachers must be a multiple of 19 (because 18 + 1 = 19). Only choice (C) divides by 19 evenly: 418 ÷ 19 = 22.

3. How many seconds are there in one day?
    A. 1,440
    B. 3,600
    C. 10,080
    **D. 86,400**

The correct answer is (D), 86,400. We know there are 60 seconds in each minute, and 60 minutes in one hour, so there would be 60 × 60 = 3,600 seconds in an hour. We know there are 24 hours in a day, so there are 3,600 × 24 = 86,400 seconds in a day.

4. When he receives his weekly paycheck, Craig deposits 20% of the money in a savings account. This week, he deposited $205.20. How much was his weekly paycheck?
    A. $225.20
    **B. $1,026.00**
    C. $1,231.20
    D. $4,104.00

The correct answer is (B), $1,026.00. 20% is equal to $\frac{1}{5}$, so that means that $205.20 is $\frac{1}{5}$ of Craig's total paycheck. Multiply by five to find the total paycheck amount: $205.20 × 5 = $1,026.00.

5. If there are approximately 3.785 L in a gallon, how many mL are in a half-gallon (to the nearest mL)?
    **A. 1,893**
    B. 2,839
    C. 3,785
    D. 7,570

The correct answer is (A), 1,893. There are 1,000 mL in a litre, so there are 3.785 × 1,000 = 3,785 mL in a gallon. Dividing this by two will give us the number of mL in a half-gallon: 3,785 ÷ 2 = 1,892.5, which, rounded to the nearest mL, is 1,893.

6. William has gotten an average score of 85 on his last three tests. If he scores a 97 on his next test, by how many points will his average test score increase?
    **A. 3**
    B. 6
    C. 9
    D. 12

The correct answer is (A), 3. If William scored an average of 85 on three tests, the sum of his scores was 85 × 3 = 255. If his next test score is a 97, that will bring his total score up to 255 + 97 = 352. Averaged over four tests, this is 352 ÷ 4 = 88. So, William's average would increase by 88 − 85 = 3 points.

7. Which number comes next in the following sequence? 1, 3, 7, 15, 31...
    A. 43
    B. 57
    **C. 63**
    D. 71

The correct answer is (C), 63. Each term is worked out by multiplying the previous term by 2 and adding 1 (e.g., $1 \times 2 + 1 = 3, 3 \times 2 + 1 = 7$, etc.). Performing this to the final term gives $31 \times 2 + 1 = 63$.

8. 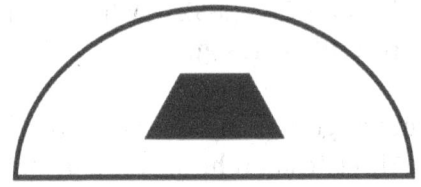 is to

as

**is to**

**A.**

B.

C.

D.

The correct answer is (A). In the first two images in the question, the second image results from rotating the outer shape (semicircle) 90° counterclockwise and rotating the inner shape (trapezoid) 90° clockwise. So, we need to find the answer choice that rotates the second image's outer shape (trapezoid) 90° counterclockwise and its inner shape (triangle) 90° clockwise. This corresponds with choice (A).

9. Two positive integers have a product of 72 and a difference of 21. What is their sum?
    - A. 17
    - B. 18
    - **C. 27**
    - D. 34

The correct answer is (C), 27. The factor pairs of 72 are 1 and 72, 2 and 36, 3 and 24, 4 and 18, 6 and 12, and 8 and 9. The only pair whose difference is 21 is 3 and 24. The sum of these two integers is 27.

10. What is the value of $2 \times 5^2 - (3 - 6) + (10 \div 2)$?
    - A. 28
    - B. 52
    - **C. 58**
    - D. 108

The correct answer is (C), 58. Use BEMDAS (Brackets, Exponents, Multiplication/Division, Addition/Subtraction) to remember the right order of operations. First, simplify the expressions inside the brackets.

$$2 \times 5^2 - (3 - 6) + (10 \div 2) =$$
$$2 \times 5^2 - (-3) + 5$$

Next, simplify the exponent.

$$2 \times 5^2 - (-3) + 5 =$$
$$2 \times 25 - (-3) + 5$$

Then, multiply.

$$2 \times 25 - (-3) + 5 =$$
$$50 - (-3) + 5$$

Finally, add and subtract from left to right.

$$50 - (-3) + 5 =$$
$$50 + 3 + 5 = 58$$

11. Kristin goes shopping during a storewide 25% off sale. She pays $41.70 for a pair of jeans and $21.00 for a shirt. How much more would Kristin have spent if she had paid full-price for these items?
    A. $15.68
    **B. $20.90**
    C. $47.03
    D. $83.60

The correct answer is (B), $20.90. Kristin paid a total of $41.70 + $21.00 = $62.70. This was $100\% - 25\% = 75\%$, or $\frac{3}{4}$, of the full price. The question asks for the value of those 25 % savings, which is equal to $\frac{1}{4}$ of the full price. Therefore, we can take what Kristin paid ($\frac{3}{4}$ of the full price) and divide it by 3 to find the value of $\frac{1}{4}$ of the full price. $62.70 ÷ 3 = $20.90, so Kristin would have paid $20.90 more if she had paid full-price.

12. Which of the following numbers has the greatest value?
    A. 0.05
    **B.** $\frac{3}{50}$
    C. 4%
    D. $0.06^2$

The correct answer is (B), $\frac{3}{50}$. Convert each answer choice to a decimal to make them easier to compare. Choice (A) is already a decimal, 0.05. In choice (B), $\frac{3}{50} = \frac{6}{100}$, which is equal to 0.06. In choice (C), 4% is equal to 0.04. In choice (D), $0.06^2 = 0.06 \times 0.06 = 0.0036$. The largest of these decimals is 0.06, choice (B).

13. After every 40 minutes of work, Hugo takes a 5-minute break. If Hugo starts working at 8:00 AM, how long will he have spent working by 11:00 AM?
    A. 2 hours
    B. 2 hours and 20 minutes

**C. 2 hours and 40 minutes**
D. 3 hours

The correct answer is (C), 2 hours and 40 minutes. From 8:00 to 11:00, there are three hours, which is equal to $3 \times 60 = 180$ minutes. Out of every 45 minutes, Hugo spends 40 minutes working and 5 minutes on break. Set up a proportion to compare Hugo's working minutes to his total minutes.

$$\frac{40}{45} = \frac{x}{180}$$
$$45x = 40(180)$$
$$45x = 7{,}200$$
$$x = 160$$

Between 8:00 and 11:00, Hugo worked for 160 minutes. To convert this to hours, divide by 60. 60 can go into 160 twice ($60 \times 2 = 120$) with 40 minutes left over ($160 - 120 = 40$), so Hugo worked for 2 hours and 40 minutes.

14. Expressed as a decimal, $\frac{9}{36}$ is equal to
    A. 0.02
    B. 0.09
    **C. 0.25**
    D. 0.9

The correct answer is (C), 0.25. It can help to begin by reducing the fraction to lowest terms:

$\frac{9}{36} = \frac{1}{4}$. Now, you want an equivalent fraction that has a denominator that is a power of 10. In this case, the lowest possible denominator that is a power of 10 is 100, so the fraction becomes $\frac{25}{100}$. Twenty-five hundredths written as a decimal is 0.25.

15. A certain three-digit number has digits that are all unique and sum to 10. What is the difference between the greatest and least possible values of this number?
    A. 136
    B. 462
    C. 774
    D. 910

The correct answer is (C), 774. First, let's determine the largest possible value. The largest digit for the hundreds place would be 9. Since the digits must all be unique and add up to 10, the other digits must be 1 and 0 (since 9 + 1 + 0 = 10). Since the number is even, we know that the 1 cannot go in the ones place, so the number must be 910. Now, let's find the smallest possible value. The smallest possible value for the hundreds place is 1, meaning the digits of the tens and ones places must sum to 9 to make the total for all digits 10. Work through each possibility, starting with the smallest possible value for the tens place. If 0 were in the tens place, the number would be

109. This is an odd number, so it cannot be correct. The tens digit cannot be a 1 since there is already a 1 in the hundreds place. If 2 were in the tens place, the number would be 127. This is odd, so it cannot be correct. If 3 were in the tens place, the number would be 136. This is an even number with three unique digits that sum to 10, so it works as our lowest possible value. Therefore, the difference between the greatest and least possible values is $910 - 136 = 774$.

16. In a group of 30 people, 14 speak French and 26 speak English. If everyone in the group speaks at least one of these languages, how many group members speak both French and English?
    A. 4
    **B. 10**
    C. 12
    D. 16

The correct answer is (B), 10. $14 + 26 = 40$ people speak French or English, which is more than the 30 people in the group. That means that $40 - 30 = 10$ of them must speak both languages.

17. If the perimeter of a square was doubled, its area would increase by a factor of
    A. 2
    **B. 4**

C. 6
D. 8

The correct answer is (B), 4. The perimeter of a square is always equal to four times the length of one side, since all 4 sides of the square are equal in length. Let's call the length of one side of the original square $s$. If the perimeter is doubled, the length of each side has also been doubled, so each side is now $2s$. The area of a square is the length of its side squared, or $A = s^2$. If the side length has doubled to $2s$, then the area of the enlarged square is $A = (2s)^2$, which simplifies to $A = 4s^2$, four times greater than the original area.

18. A car travelling down a road at an average speed of 50 km per hour takes 2 hours to complete a trip. How much shorter would the trip have been if the car had instead travelled at an average speed of 60 km per hour?
    
    **A. 20 minutes**
    B. 40 minutes
    C. 1 hour and 20 minutes
    D. 1 hour and 40 minutes

The correct answer is (A), 20 minutes. If it took the car 2 hours to complete the trip at 50 km per hour, the total distance of the trip was $50 \times 2 = 100$ km. Covering the same distance at a speed of 60 km per hour would take $100 \div$

$60 = 1\frac{2}{3}$ hours, which is equal to 1 hour and 40 minutes. Subtracting this from 2 hours gives a difference in travel time of 20 minutes.

19. In an office of 50 employees, 29 of them drive to work, 6% ride a bike to work, and the rest use public transportation to get to work. If one employee is randomly selected from this group, what is the probability that the employee gets to work using public transportation?

    A. $\frac{1}{6}$
    B. $\frac{3}{10}$
    C. $\frac{9}{25}$
    D. $\frac{9}{16}$

The correct answer is (C), $\frac{9}{25}$. 6% of the 50 employees ride a bike, which is $50 \times 0.06 = 3$ employees. Adding this to the number of employees that drive gives us $3 + 29 = 32$ employees that do not use public transportation. That means $50 - 32 = 18$ employees use public transportation. Therefore, the probability of a randomly selected employee using public transportation is $\frac{18}{50}$, which reduces to $\frac{9}{25}$.

20. 80% of 60 is equal to 30% of what number?
    A. 18

B. 40
C. 66
**D. 160**

The correct answer is (D), 160. 60% of 80 is $80 \times 0.6 = 48$. Use the percent formula to find out what 48 is 30% off.

$$\frac{\%}{100} = \frac{part}{whole}$$
$$\frac{30}{100} = \frac{48}{x}$$
$$30x = 100(48)$$
$$30x = 4{,}800$$
$$x = 160$$

21. A recipe for 12 cupcakes calls for $1\frac{1}{4}$ cups of flour. How many cups of flour would be needed to bake three dozen cupcakes?

    A. $2\frac{1}{2}$
    B. $2\frac{3}{4}$
    C. $3\frac{1}{2}$
    **D. $3\frac{3}{4}$**

The correct answer is (D), $3\frac{3}{4}$. If one dozen (12) cupcakes require $1\frac{1}{4}$ cups of flour, then three dozen cupcakes will require three times as much flour. $1\frac{1}{4} \times 3 = 3\frac{3}{4}$.

22. When 5 is divided by 0.04, the quotient is

    A. 0.2

B. 0.5
C. 12.5
**D. 125**

The correct answer is (D), 125. Since you can't use a calculator, it may be easier to perform this division by first converting 0.04 to a fraction, which is $\frac{4}{100}$. Remember, dividing by a fraction is the same thing as multiplying by its reciprocal, so $\frac{5}{1} \div \frac{4}{100} = \frac{5}{1} \times \frac{100}{4} = \frac{500}{4} = 125$.

23. What is the average of $\frac{2}{5}$ and $\frac{4}{9}$?

    A. $\frac{2}{15}$
    **B.** $\frac{19}{45}$
    C. $\frac{3}{7}$
    D. $\frac{2}{3}$

The correct answer is (B), $\frac{19}{45}$. To find the average of two terms, add them and divide by the number of terms. To add $\frac{2}{5}$ and $\frac{4}{9}$, we'll need a common denominator. The least common multiple of 5 and 9 is 45, so convert both fractions to equivalent fractions with the common denominator: $\frac{2}{5} = \frac{18}{45}$ and $\frac{4}{9} = \frac{20}{45}$. Now we can add: $\frac{18}{45} + \frac{20}{45} = \frac{38}{45}$. Dividing this by the number of terms (2) gives $\frac{38}{45} \div 2 = \frac{19}{45}$.

24. At a cafe, Lisa pays $5.35 for a cup of coffee and a donut. Anita pays $6.95 for a cup of coffee and two donuts. What would the price of three cups of coffee be?
    A. $4.80
    B. $6.15
    **C. $11.25**
    D. $12.30

The correct answer is (C), $11.25. The only difference between Lisa's order and Anita's is that Anita bought one more donut than Lisa did. So, the difference in price between the two orders is equal to the cost of one donut. $6.95 − $5.35 = $1.60, so one donut costs $1.60. We can then subtract this from Lisa's order to find the price of one cup of coffee: $5.35 − $1.60 = $3.75. If one cup of coffee costs $3.75, then three cups of coffee costs $3.75 × 3 = $11.25.

25. $12 \times 3 - (-2) =$
    A. 12
    B. 32
    **C. 38**
    D. 60

The correct answer is (C), 38. According to the order of operations, multiplication must be done before subtraction, so $12 \times 3 - (-2) = 36 - (-2) = 36 + 2 = 38$.

26. Becky is 18 years old, which is two years more than half of Carl's age. Adam is two years older than Becky. How many years older than Adam is Carl?

   **A. 12**
   B. 14
   C. 20
   D. 32

The correct answer is (A), 12. Becky is 18, and Adam is two years older, so Adam is $18 + 2 = 20$ years old. Becky is also two years more than half of Carl's age. That means that $18 - 2 = 16$ is half of Carl's age, so Carl is $16 \times 2 = 32$ years old. Carl is $32 - 20 = 12$ years older than Adam.

27. Paul earns $45 per hour at his job. If he works for more than 40 hours in a given week, he earns overtime pay for those additional hours at a rate of 1.5 times his normal wage. How much would Paul earn if he worked 46 hours in a week?

   A. $1,935
   B. $2,070
   **C. $2,205**
   D. $3,105

The correct answer is (C), $2,205. For the first 40 hours, Paul earns $45 \times 40 = \$1,800$. For the six additional hours he worked, he earned 1.5 times his normal wage, which is $45 \times 1.5 = \$67.50$ per hour. Over six hours, this comes to

$67.50 \times 6 = \$405$. Adding these figures together gives $\$1,800 + \$405 = \$2,205$ in total weekly earnings.

28. Mei is packaging cupcakes at a bakery in boxes of six cupcakes. When she finishes filling the boxes, she has no cupcakes left over. Which of these could NOT be the number of cupcakes she started with?

    A. 162
    B. 174
    C. 186
    **D. 190**

The correct answer is (D), 190. Since there are no cupcakes left over, the number of cupcakes Mei started with must be divisible by 6. The only number among the answer choices not divisible by 6 is (D), 190. You could find this answer by testing each choice–dividing each number by 6 to determine if it comes out evenly. A time-saving trick is to remember that any number divisible by 6 must also be divisible by 2 (so it must be even) and by 3 (which means its digits add up to 3 or a multiple of 3). All of the answer choices are even, and choices (A), (B), and (C) have digits that add up to a multiple of 3. The digits of choice (D) add up to 10, so it is not divisible by 3 (and therefore not divisible by 6).

29. Troy wants to buy two books with list prices of $23.00 and $31.00. The bookstore is running a sale where if you buy one book at full price, you can buy a second book of equal or lesser value at 50% off. How much would Troy pay if he bought both books during the sale?

    A. $27.00
    B. $38.50
    **C. $42.50**
    D. $49.00

The correct answer is (C), $42.50. The sale lets you take 50% off of the lower-priced book, so the book that originally cost $23.00 would be $23.00 × 0.5 = $11.50. Adding this to the full price of the other book gives $31.00 + $11.50 = $42.50.

30. Which number comes next in the following sequence? 80, 20, 5...

    A. −10
    B. 1
    **C. 1.25**
    D. 2.5

The correct answer is (C), 1.25. Each term in the sequence is the result of dividing the previous term by 4, so the next term would be 5 ÷ 4 = 1.25.

# Chapter 12: Practice Test 3 Answers With Explanations

## Verbal Skills

1. INDICATE means the same as
    A. explore
    B. ignore
    C. promote
    **D. show**

    The correct answer is (D), show. To *indicate* means to point out or make clear. *Show* is the best match. Choice (A) is incorrect because *explore* involves investigating, not pointing out something already known. Choice (B) is incorrect because to *ignore* is to pay no attention to something, which contradicts the meaning of *indicate*. Choice (C) is incorrect because to *promote* is to encourage something, which implies more of an agenda than *indicate* does.

2. LIKE is to LOVE as DISLIKE is to
   A. mistrust
   **B. abhor**
   C. omit
   D. adore

The correct answer is (B), abhor. *Love* is a stronger degree of *like*; similarly, *abhor* (hate) is a stronger degree of *dislike*. Choice (A) is incorrect because *mistrust* means to be suspicious, which could be related to *dislike* but is not a stronger degree of the same meaning. Choice (C) is incorrect because *omit* means to leave out, which is not a stronger degree of *dislike*. Choice (D) is incorrect because *adore* is a synonym for *love*, which relates to the first part of the analogy rather than the second.

3. CONSENSUS means the same as
   **A. agreement**
   B. dissension
   C. happiness
   D. uncertainty

The correct answer is (A), agreement. *Consensus* occurs when everyone in a group agrees on something, so *agreement* is the best match. Choice (B) is incorrect because *dissension* means disagreement, which is the opposite of *consensus*. Choice (C) is incorrect because *happiness* refers to a feeling, not a shared opinion. Choice (D) is incorrect because a group in agreement with each other does not imply *uncertainty*, or being unsure.

4. HINDER means the same as
   A. allow
   B. aid
   C. regret
   **D. prevent**

The correct answer is (D), prevent. *Hinder* means to make something more difficult. *Prevent* is the best match. Choice (A) is incorrect because hindering something means not allowing it to happen easily. Choice (B) is incorrect because to *aid*, or help, is the opposite of *hinder*. Choice (C) is incorrect because *regret* means to feel sorry about something that has been done, which is not a synonym for *hinder*.

5. OPEN is to CLOSE as BEGIN is to
   A. shut
   B. commence
   **C. terminate**
   D. unseal

The correct answer is (C), terminate. *Open* and *close* are opposites, so you need the opposite of *begin* to complete the analogy. The best choice is *terminate*, which means to stop or end. Choice (A) is incorrect because *shut* is a synonym for *close*, so it relates to the first part of the analogy rather than the second. Choice (B) is incorrect because *commence* is a synonym for *begin* rather than its opposite. Choice (D) is incorrect because *unseal* can be a synonym for *open*, which relates to the first part of the analogy but not the second.

6. MODIFY means the same as
    A. maintain
    B. calculate
    C. predict
    **D. alter**

The correct answer is (D), alter. *Modify* means to change, which is also the meaning of *alter*. Choice (A) is incorrect because to *maintain* something would be to keep it the same, which is the opposite of *modify*. Choice (B) is incorrect because to *calculate* is to determine something mathematically, which is not a good match for *modify*. Choice (C) is incorrect because *predict* means to guess what will happen in the future, which is not a good match for *modify*.

7. PRECEDE is the opposite of
    A. predate
    **B. follow**
    C. exit
    D. undergo

The correct answer is (B), follow. *Precede* means to come before, so the opposite would be to come after, or *follow*. Choice (A) is incorrect because *predate* is a synonym, not an opposite, for *precede*. Choice (C) is incorrect because *exit* means to leave, which is not the opposite of *precede*. Choice (D) is incorrect because *undergo* means to experience, which is not the opposite of *precede*.

8. OBVIOUS means the same as
    **A. clear**
    B. vague
    C. foolish
    D. unaware

The correct answer is (A), clear. Something *obvious* is easy to see or understand. *Clear* is the best match. Choice (B) is incorrect because *vague* means unclear, which is the opposite of *obvious*. Choice (C) is incorrect because *foolish* means lacking sense, which is different from *obvious*. Choice (D) is incorrect because to be *unaware* is to be ignorant of something, which is not a good match for *obvious*.

9. MINIMIZE means the same as
    A. prolong
    **B. reduce**
    C. close
    D. continue

The correct answer is (B), reduce. To *minimize* is to make something smaller, so *reduce* is the best fit. Choice (A) is incorrect because *prolong* means to make something last longer, which is the opposite of *minimize*. Choice (C) is incorrect because *minimize* means to lessen something, not stop it altogether, as *close* would indicate. Choice (D) is incorrect because *continue* means to keep going, which does not fit the meaning of *minimize*.

10. A DOCILE person is
    A. lazy
    B. bored
    C. assertive
    **D. compliant**

The correct answer is (D), compliant. A *docile* person is submissive and accepts instruction from others. The best match is *compliant*, which means obedient. Choices (A) and (B) are incorrect because a *docile* person is not necessarily *lazy* or *bored*. Choice (C) is incorrect because *assertive* is the opposite of *docile*.

11. DISCREET means the same as
    A. heedless
    B. disrespectful
    **C. unobtrusive**
    D. brazen

The correct answer is (C), unobtrusive. To do something discreetly is to be careful not to draw attention. *Unobtrusive*, which means not attracting attention, is the best fit. Choice (A) is incorrect because *heedless* means careless, which is the opposite of *discreet*. Choice (B) is incorrect because to be *discreet* does not mean to lack respect. Choice (D) is incorrect because *brazen* means bold or unashamed, which is not a match for *discreet*.

12. PACK is to WOLVES as ORCHESTRA is to
    A. violin
    **B. musicians**
    C. symphony
    D. conductor

The correct answer is (B), musicians. A *pack* is a group of wolves, just as an *orchestra* is a group of *musicians*. Choice (A) is incorrect because a single *violin* is just one of many instruments that can make up an orchestra, whereas the plural *wolves* are the members that entirely constitute the *pack*. Choice (C) is incorrect because a *symphony* is music the orchestra may produce, but it does not describe the orchestra's members. Choice (D) is incorrect because the *conductor* is the single leader of the *orchestra*, not all of its members.

13. COMPOUND means the same as
    **A. aggravate**
    B. separate
    C. clarify
    D. improve

The correct answer is (A), aggravate. As a verb, *compound* means to make something worse, so *aggravate* is the best fit. Choice (B) is incorrect because compounding adds to the negative aspects of a situation; it does not involve separating. Choice (C) is incorrect because compounding a situation complicates it; it doesn't *clarify*, or make it more clear. Choice (D) is incorrect because *compound* has a negative connotation, and *improve* indicates positive change.

14. A CONTROVERSIAL issue is
    A. unquestionable
    B. listless
    **C. disputed**
    D. uplifting

The correct answer is (C), disputed. A *controversial* issue is one that leads to a lot of disagreement, so *disputed* is the best fit. Choice (A) is incorrect because a controversial issue raises many questions. Choice (B) is incorrect because *listless* means dull, and controversy often evokes strong feelings. Choice (D) is incorrect because something *uplifting* makes people feel happier, and this is typically not the result of a controversial issue.

15. RELINQUISH means the same as
    A. grasp
    **B. abdicate**
    C. undertake
    D. challenge

The correct answer is (B), abdicate. Both *relinquish* and *abdicate* mean to give something up. Choice (A) is incorrect because to *grasp*, or hold onto, something is the opposite of *relinquish*. Choice (C) is incorrect because to *undertake* is to begin or attempt, which is not a good fit for *relinquish*. Choice (D) is incorrect because *challenge* means to dispute or compete, which is not a good fit for *relinquish*.

# Spatial Ability

**1)**

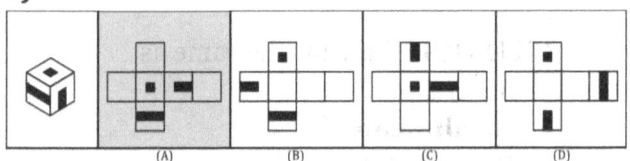

**2)**

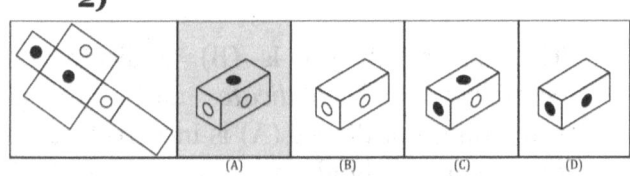

**3)**

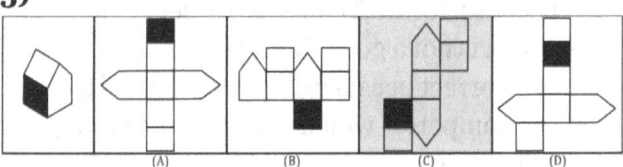

**4)**

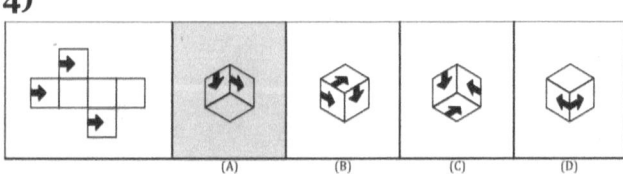

**5)**

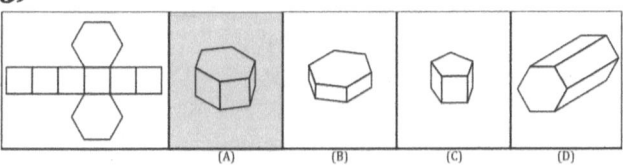

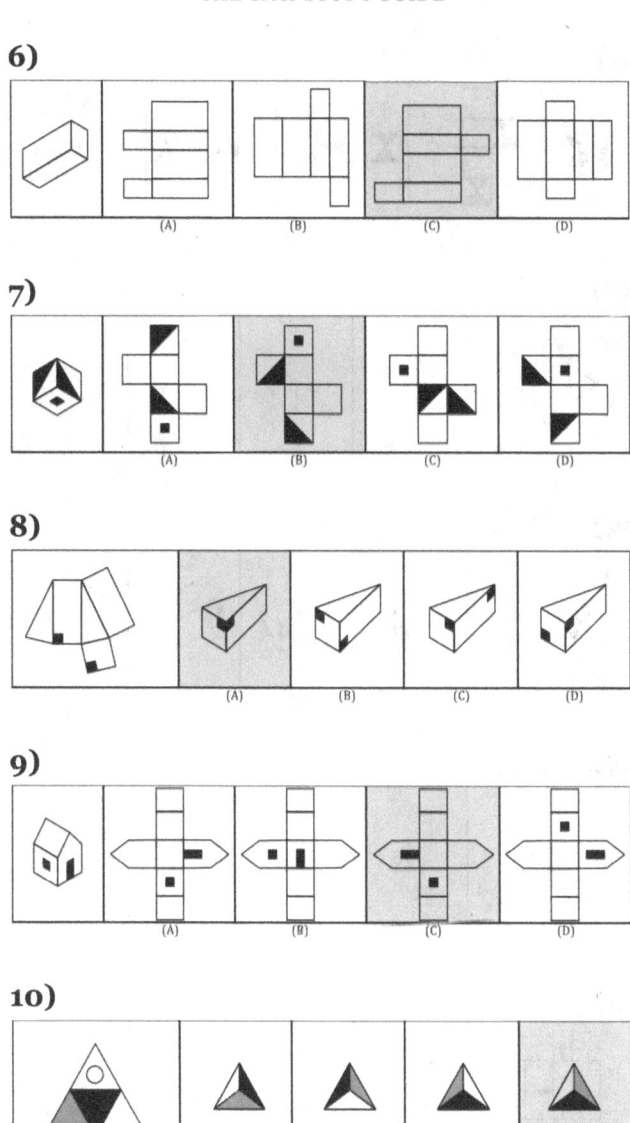

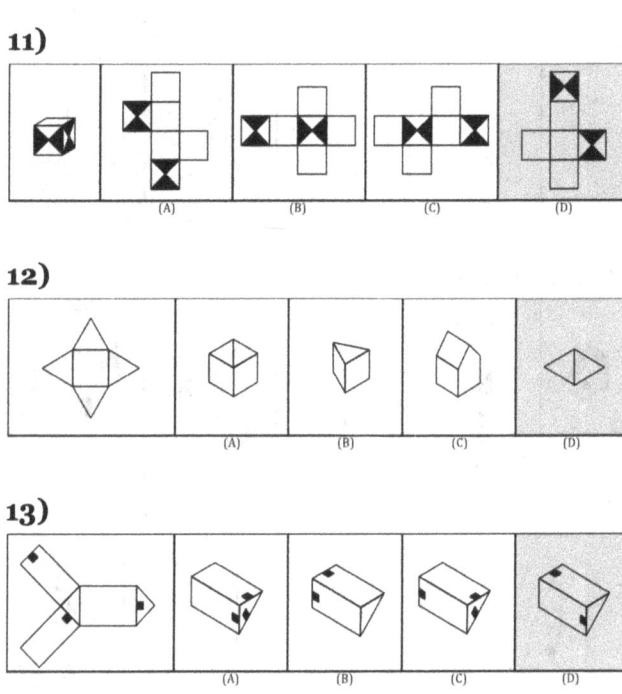

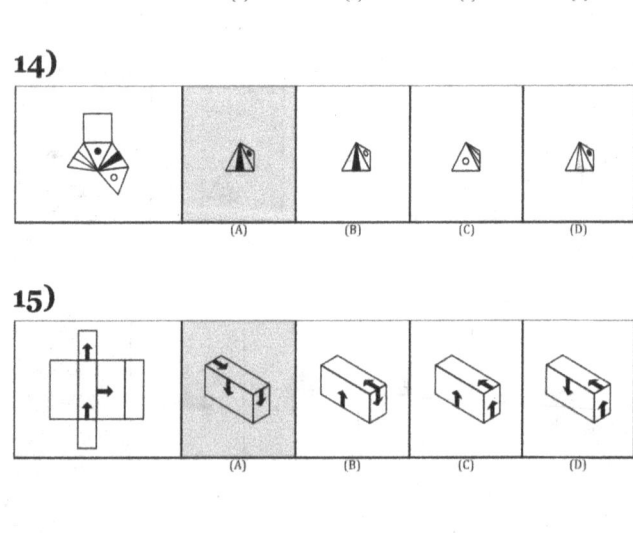

# Problem Solving

1. A teacher puts a class of 29 students into groups of two or three students. What would be the smallest number of groups possible?
     A. 8
     B. 9
     **C. 10**
     D. 11

   The correct answer is (C), 10. To get the smallest number of groups, we want to have as many groups of 3 as possible. Three divides into 29 nine times ($3 \times 9 = 27$), with two students left over ($29 - 27 = 2$). So in this arrangement, there will be nine groups of three and one group of two, for a total of $9 + 1 = 10$ groups.

2. If $a = -3$, what is the value of $3a^2 + 2a - 4$?
     A. $-91$
     B. $-37$
     **C. 17**
     D. 71

   The correct answer is (C), 17. Plug $-3$ in for $a$ in the given expression.

   $$3a^2 + 2a - 4$$
   $$3(-3)^2 + 2(-3) - 4 =$$
   $$3(9) - 6 - 4 =$$

$$27 - 10 = 17$$

3. How many hours are there in one leap year?
    - A. 8,064
    - B. 8,736
    - C. 8,760
    - **D. 8,784**

The correct answer is (D), 8,784. There are 24 hours in each day and 366 days in a leap year, for a total of 24 × 366 = 8,784 hours.

4. Where $a, b$, and $c$, are all positive numbers, $a$ is twice as large as $b$, and $c$ is equal to the product of $a$ and $b$, then half of $c$ is equal to
    - A. $b$
    - **B. $b^2$**
    - C. $\frac{b}{2}$
    - D. $-b$

The correct answer is (B), $b^2$. First, let's create equations to express the given information. We know that "$a$ is twice as large as $b$," so $a = 2b$. We also know that "$c$ is equal to the product of $a$ and $b$," so $c = ab$. The question is asking for the value of "half of $c$," or $\frac{c}{2}$. Since $c = ab, \frac{c}{2} = \frac{ab}{2}$. All the answer choices include a $b$ so we need to solve in terms of $b$ (getting rid of the $a$). Since $a = 2b$, we can replace $a$ with $2b$, so $\frac{ab}{2} = \frac{(2b)b}{2} = \frac{2b^2}{2}$, which simplifies to $b^2$.

5. A grocery store sells Red Delicious apples for $5.50 per kg and Honeycrisp apples for $8.60 per kg. If Dan buys 2.5 kg of apples, how much more would it cost to buy Honeycrisp apples than Red Delicious apples?
   A. $3.10
   B. $6.20
   **C. $7.75**
   D. $13.75

The correct answer is (C), $7.75. The difference in price per kg of apples is $8.60 − $5.50 = $3.10. So, for 2.5 kg of apples, this becomes a difference of $3.10 × 2.5 = $7.75.

6. How many numbers less than 100 are multiples of both 5 and 3?
   **A. 6**
   B. 15
   C. 20
   D. 26

The correct answer is (A), 6. Multiples of 5 always end in either a 0 or a 5. Those that are also multiples of 3 are the multiples of 15 (3 × 5), which are 15, 30, 45, 60, 75, and 90. That list contains six numbers.

7. Which number comes next in the following sequence? 2, 10, 40, 120, 240...
   **A. 240**

B. 360
C. 400
D. 480

The correct answer is (A), 240. Each term is multiplied by a factor that decreases by 1 each time, so 2 is multiplied by 5 to get 10, 10 is multiplied by 4 to get 40, 40 is multiplied by 3 to get 120, and 120 is multiplied by 2 to get 240. The next step would be to multiply 240 by 1, which equals 240.

8. A course allows a maximum of 40 students to enroll. If 32 of the spots are currently filled, what percentage of the spots are still available?
    A. 8%
    **B. 20%**
    C. 40%
    D. 80%

The correct answer is (B), 20%. If 32 spots are filled, then $40 - 32 = 8$ spots are still available. $8 \div 40 = 0.2 = 20\%$ of the spots are still available.

THE CFAT STUDY GUIDE

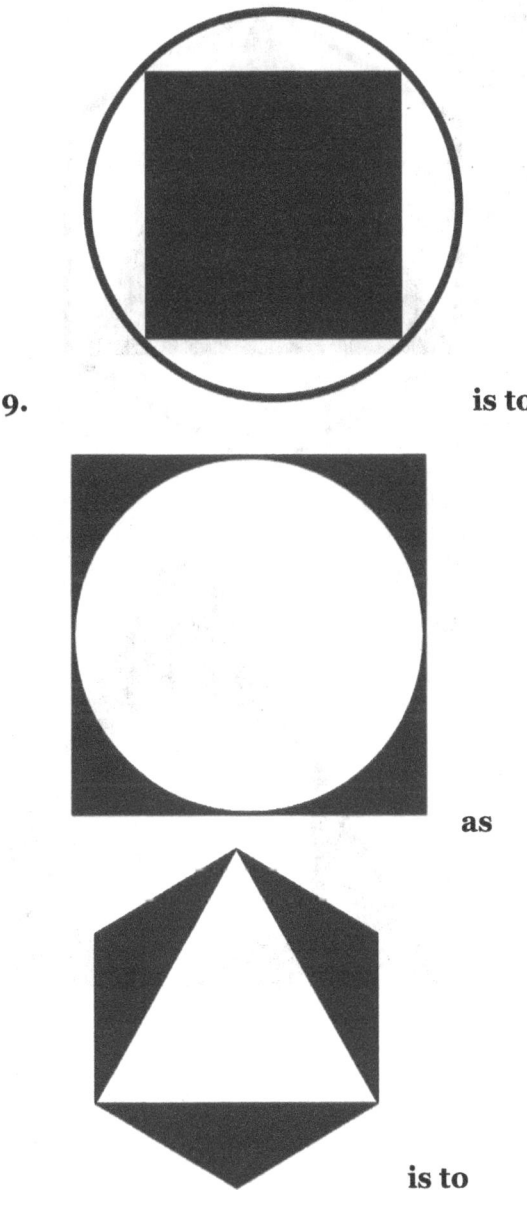

9. is to

as

is to

193

FRED WINSTONE

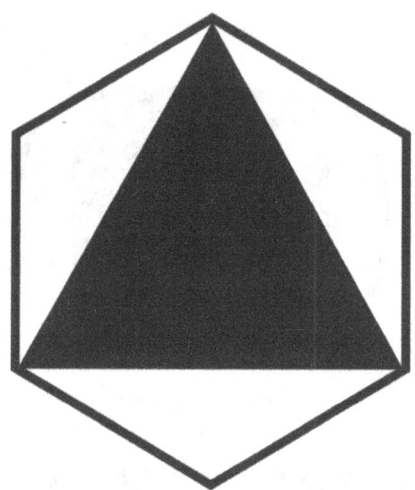

A.

B.

**C.**

**D.**

The correct answer is (D). In the first pair of images, the centre shape (the black square) stays the same in the second image, and the outer shape (the white circle) gets smaller and becomes the new inner shape. The third image shows a white triangle inside a black hexagon, so we need to complete the analogy with the same white triangle with a small black hexagon inside. This matches choice (D).

10. Which of the following is NOT equal to the other three?
    A. $0.5^2$
    B. $\frac{1}{4}$
    **C. 0.2**
    D. 25%

The correct answer is (C), 0.2. The other three choices are all equal to 0.25, so choice (C) is the only one that does not match.

11. What is the value of $(3 - 6)^2 + 2 \times 5 - 1$?
    A. 0
    **B. 18**
    C. 44
    D. 54

The correct answer is (B), 18. Use BEMDAS (Brackets, Exponents, Multiplication/Division, Addition/Subtraction) to follow the correct order of operations.

$$(3 - 6)^2 + 2 \times 5 - 1 =$$
$$(-3)^2 + 2 \times 5 - 1 =$$
$$9 + 2 \times 5 - 1 =$$
$$9 + 10 - 1 =$$
$$19 - 1 = 18$$

12. Evelyn purchased a sofa on sale for 30% off. If she paid $560, how much money did she save compared to the regular price?
    A. $168
    **B. $240**
    C. $392
    D. $800

The correct answer is (B), $240. We are looking for the dollar amount of the 30% savings. Let $x$ represent this amount. The regular price of the sofa would therefore be $560 + x$. Use the percent formula to solve for $x$.

$$\frac{percent}{100} = \frac{part}{whole}$$
$$\frac{30}{100} = \frac{x}{560 + x}$$
$$30(560 + x) = 100x$$
$$16,800 + 30x = 100x$$
$$16,800 = 70x$$
$$240 = x$$

Evelyn saved $240 by purchasing the sofa on sale.

13. Michelle can decorate three cupcakes in five minutes. At this rate, how many cupcakes can she decorate in one hour?
    A. 24
    B. 30
    **C. 36**
    D. 48

The correct answer is (C), 36. Set up a proportion to solve.

$$\frac{3 \; cupcakes}{5 \; minutes} = \frac{x \; cupcakes}{60 \; minutes}$$
$$3(60) = 5x$$
$$180 = 5x$$
$$36 = x$$

Michelle can decorate 36 cupcakes in one hour.

14. Four friends have dinner together at a restaurant. Their bill comes to $96. They decide on splitting the bill evenly and leaving a 20% tip. How much does each person pay?
    A. $19.20
    B. $24.20
    **C. $28.80**
    D. $29.00

The correct answer is (C), $28.80. The bill comes to $96, and they leave a 20% tip, so the total with the tip will be 120% of the $96 bill. This comes to $96 × 1.2 = $115.20. Splitting that evenly among four people gives $115.20 ÷ 4 = $28.80.

15. What is the smallest positive four-digit integer that is divisible by 3?
    A. 1,000
    **B. 1,002**
    C. 1,012
    D. 1,200

The correct answer is (B), 1,002. The smallest possible four-digit number will have a one in the thousands place and zeroes in the hundreds and tens places. This leaves choices (A) and (B). Since (A) does not divide evenly by three but (B) does (1,002 ÷ 3 = 334), the answer is (B).

16. Calculate the probability of rolling a number greater than 2 on a standard 6-sided dice?
    A. $\frac{1}{6}$
    B. $\frac{1}{3}$
    C. $\frac{1}{2}$
    **D. $\frac{2}{3}$**

The correct answer is (D), $\frac{2}{3}$. There are 4 numbers greater than 2 on a dice (out of 6 numbers total), so the probability, or chance of rolling a number greater than 2 is $\frac{4}{6}$, which reduces to $\frac{2}{3}$.

17. Nick is installing square tiles that are 60 cm long on the floor of a rectangular room that measures 5.4 meters by 6 meters. How many tiles would he need to cover the entire floor?
    A. 80
    **B. 90**
    C. 110
    D. 120

The correct answer is (B), 90. There are 100 cm in each meter, so the room measures 540 cm by 600 cm. Along the side that measures 540 cm, Nick will need 540 ÷ 60 = 9 tiles, and along the side that measures 600 cm, he will need 600 ÷ 60 = 10 tiles. The floor measures 9 tiles by 10 tiles, so filling the area with tiles will require 9 × 10 = 90 tiles.

18. Teresa leaves home at 7:20 and drives for 42 km at an average speed of 70 km per hour. What time does she arrive at her destination?
    A. 7:36
    **B. 7:56**
    C. 8:02
    D. 8:30

The correct answer is (B), 7:56. She travels 70 km per hour, which is equal to 70 km in 60 minutes. Set up a proportion to find out how many minutes her drive takes.
$$\frac{70\ km}{60\ minutes} = \frac{42\ km}{x\ minutes}$$
$$70x = 60(42)$$
$$70x = 2{,}520$$
$$x = 36$$
So, Teresa spent 36 minutes driving. She left at 7:20, so adding 36 minutes gives us 7:56.

19. $\frac{2}{5}$ of the pens in Kaylee's bag are blue, and the rest are black. What percentage of her pens are black?

   A. 20%
   B. 40%
   **C. 60%**
   D. 80%

The correct answer is (C), 60%. If $\frac{2}{5}$ of the pens are blue, then $\frac{3}{5}$ are black. $3 \div 5 = 0.6$, so, this equals 60% of the pens.

20. If 25% of a number works out to 60, what is $\frac{1}{3}$ of the number?

   A. 5
   B. 20
   C. 65
   **D. 80**

The correct answer is (D), 80. 25% is equal to $\frac{1}{4}$, so we know that 60 is $\frac{1}{4}$ of the number. We can find the number by multiplying by 4, giving us $60 \times 4 = 240$. Divide to find $\frac{1}{3}$ of this number: $240 \div 3 = 80$.

21. A gymnastics class costs $80 per month per student. If more than one student from the same family enrolls, this monthly price is reduced by $5 per student. How much would

it cost for two students from the same family to take the gymnastics class for six months?

A. $450
B. $750
**C. $900**
D. $950

The correct answer is (C), $900. Since two students from the same family are enrolled, the discount applies, so each student will pay $80 − $5 = $75 per month. There are two of them, so that is $75 × 2 = $150 per month for both students. Over six months, this becomes a total of $150 × 6 = $900.

22. The average of the numbers $a$ and $b$ is 23. The average of $a$, $b$, & $c$ is 27. What is the value of $c$?

    A. 4
    **B. 35**
    C. 42
    D. 58

The correct answer is (B), 35. Use the average formula to solve. Start with what we know of the average of $a$ and $b$.

$$Average = \frac{sum\ of\ terms}{number\ of\ terms}$$
$$23 = \frac{a+b}{2}$$
$$46 = a+b$$

So, the sum of $a$ and $b$ is 46. We can use that to find the value of $c$ using the average formula and the given average of all three terms.

$$Average = \frac{sum\ of\ terms}{number\ of\ terms}$$

$$27 = \frac{a+b+c}{3}$$

$$27 = \frac{46+c}{3}$$

$$81 = 46 + c$$

$$35 = c$$

23. Jared needs the brake pads and rotors replaced for both rear wheels of his car. An automotive repair shop charges $110 per wheel for rotors, and brake pads are sold as a set for two wheels for $85. In addition, they charge $100 per hour for labour. If the repair takes 45 minutes for the shop to complete, what will Jared's total cost be?

    A. $295
    **B. $380**
    C. $405
    D. $465

The correct answer is (B), $380. Rotors are $110 per wheel, so the cost will be $110 × 2 = $220 for two wheels. Adding this to the cost of the set of brake pads gives $220 + $85 = $305 for the parts. Labour costs $100 per hour, and the repair took 45 minutes, which is equal to 45 ÷ 60 = 0.75 of an hour. This gives a labour cost of $100 \times 0.75 = \$75$. Adding this to the cost of the parts gives a total of $\$305 + \$75 = \$380$.

24. Which of the following has the smallest value?
    A. 0.05
    **B.** $\frac{2}{50}$
    C. $0.3^2$
    D. $\frac{1}{10}$

The correct answer is (B), $\frac{2}{50}$. Convert all of the answer choices into decimals to make them easier to compare. Choice (A) is already a decimal, 0.05. Choice (B) is $\frac{2}{50}$. Multiplying both the top and bottom of the fraction by 2 gives $\frac{4}{100}$. Expressed as a decimal, this is 0.04. In choice (C), $0.3^2 = 0.09$. Converting choice (D), $\frac{1}{10}$ to a fraction gives 0.1. The smallest of these values is choice (B), 0.04.

25. The hardcover version of a book sells for $20, while the paperback version sells for $12. What is the percent savings for buying the paperback version instead of the hardcover?
    A. 8%
    B. 25%
    **C. 40%**
    D. 60%

The correct answer is (C), 40%. Opting for the paperback version gives a savings of $20 − $12 = $8. This is a discount of $\frac{8}{20} = 0.4 = 40\%$ off of the hardcover price.

26. Riley has a rock collection with a total of 36 rocks. The ratio of igneous to metamorphic to sedimentary rocks in her collection is 3:5:1. How many metamorphic rocks does she have?
    A. 5
    B. 7
    C. 12
    **D. 20**

The correct answer is (D), 20. $3 + 5 + 1 = 9$, so the given ratio tells us the distribution of each type of rock within each set of 9 rocks. There are a total of 36 rocks, so there are $36 \div 9 = 4$ sets of 9 rocks. If there are 5 metamorphic rocks in each set of 9, then there are $5 \times 4 = 20$ metamorphic rocks in the entire collection.

27. There are three children in the Davis family. The youngest is half the age of the oldest. The middle child is 7 years old and is two years older than the youngest. What is the total of all of their ages (in years)?
    A. 17
    B. 18
    **C. 22**
    D. 30

The correct answer is (C), 22. The middle child is 7, which is two years older than the youngest child, so the youngest must be $7 - 2 = 5$ years old. The youngest is half the age of the oldest, so the oldest must be $5 \times 2 = 10$. This gives a total age of $10 + 7 + 5 = 22$ years.

28. One week in February, the high temperature in Toronto was 3°C for three days, 2°C one day, 1°C for two days, and 4°C one day. What was the average daily high temperature for the week (to the nearest tenth)?

    A. 1.7°C
    B. 2.1°C
    **C. 2.4°C**
    D. 3.2°C

The correct answer is (C), 2.4°C. First, add up the total number of degrees for the week, multiplying each temperature by the number of days that experienced that temperature.

$$3(3) + 2(1) + 1(2) + 4(1) =$$
$$9 + 2 + 2 + 4 = 17$$

Then, divide this by the number of days. $17 \div 7 = 2.4$ (roundest to the nearest tenth).

29. Which number comes next in the following sequence? $-24, 12, -6 \ldots$

    A. $-3$
    **B. 3**
    C. 12
    D. 18

The correct answer is (B), 3. Each term is the result of dividing the previous term by −2, so the next term would be (−6) ÷ (−2) = 3.

30. A Canadian passport photo must measure 50 mm by 70 mm. What is the perimeter of the photo (in mm)?
    A. 120
    **B. 240**
    C. 1,200
    D. 3,500

The correct answer is (B), 240. To find the perimeter of a rectangle, simply add the lengths of the sides: 50 + 70 + 50 + 70 = 240 mm.

# Conclusion

Congratulations! You made it through this CFAT review. If you read this entire book, you've reviewed all three CFAT sections and completed three full-length practice tests. You've also been equipped with strategies to help you find success. Now that you know what to expect on the CFAT, you can continue to prepare.

As your testing appointment nears, make the most of your study time. If you've taken the practice tests, use your results to guide your preparation. Whether or not you scored well on the practice tests, they are very useful for helping you see which areas you most need to study. As you continue to study, prioritize the sections where you need the most work. As you review the practice tests, be sure to read the answers and explanations thoroughly, even for the questions you got right. They can help you better understand the material.

While it is important to do your best on all three subtests of the CFAT, if you need to prioritize your study time, it can also help to consider which subtests are most important for your career goals. While the CFAT tests broad skills that are applicable in many areas, some positions rely more heavily on specific skills than others. For instance, communications-related jobs will require greater verbal skills, while the problem-solving test will be more important for more technical positions.

If you have a particular job or area of interest, focus on doing well on the subtests that pertain to that role. You can talk to your recruiter about your goals, and they can tell you which subtests matter most for the positions you are interested in.

Getting ready for the CFAT can be stressful, but we want to help you do your best without getting overwhelmed. Here are some tips for time and stress management while you prepare.

- Set goals. Making small, manageable goals can help you maintain focus and feel good about your progress.
- Schedule your time. If you have your testing appointment set, work backward and figure out how much time you have to study. Then, create a schedule for yourself, setting aside blocks of time in your week for CFAT preparation. Plan out how you will use your study time, prioritizing topics using the guidelines discussed above.
- Take care of yourself. When we don't take good care of our bodies and minds, it can compound the stress we are already feeling. Be sure to eat right, get enough sleep, and move your body regularly. Take care of your mental health by taking breaks with stress-relieving activities you enjoy.

If you need more information about the CFAT or want to take the official CFAT practice test, check out "What is the CFAT?" from the official CAF website at https://forces.ca/en/help-centre/#/view/27. You can also find additional study resources online, such as the helpful YouTube channel of Kyra Nankivell at https://www.youtube.com/@KyraNankivell.

Here are some final tips to help you do your best on the day of your testing appointment.

- Get a good night's sleep and have something to eat before your exam. Being well-rested and fueled will help keep your mind sharp and ready.
- Give yourself enough time to get ready in the morning and arrive early at the testing site. Rushing to get there on time will make you even more stressed, and arriving late could mean a delay in your application process.
- While taking the test, pay attention to the time and pace yourself. Don't stress and spend too much time on any one particular question. This is especially important for Verbal Skills and Spatial Ability, where you have less than one minute per question.
- Read each question and *all* of the possible answers carefully before selecting one. Wrong answer choices often contain the most common mistakes people make. Be sure you are answering the question being asked.
- If you don't know the answer, use the process of elimination to narrow down the choices. On

the CFAT, there are no penalties for wrong answers, so you should never have an excuse to leave a question blank. Narrow it down as much as you can and take your best guess.

Thank you for studying with us! We hope that this book has made you feel prepared and confident for your CFAT. Keep studying and put in your best effort, and you will be well on your way to a rewarding career in the Canadian Forces. **If you found this book helpful, please consider leaving a positive 5\* review on Amazon.** It helps our book get noticed and get into the hands of others who could benefit from this study guide to help them prepare for the CFAT, just like you.

Best of luck on the CFAT and in all of your future endeavours!

Best wishes,

**Fred Winstone**

www.ingramcontent.com/pod-product-compliance
Lightning Source LLC
Chambersburg PA
CBHW012004090526
44590CB00026B/3867